When the Grass Turns Green

Cherished Baseball Memories of a North Carolina Sports Writer

By
Thad Mumau

2010
Parkway Publishers, Inc.
Boone, North Carolina

Cover and Author Photographs by Steve Aldridge
Model for the cover photo Andrew Henrickson

Library of Congress Cataloging-in-Publication Data

Mumau, Thad.
When the grass turns green : cherished baseball memories of a North Carolina sports writer / by Thad Mumau.
p. cm.
Includes bibliographical references.
Summary: "When the Grass Turns Green is Thad Mumau's memoir depicting his life-long love of baseball which started when his father brought him a baseball glove. He later became a baseball player and a sports writer"--Provided by publisher.
 ISBN 978-1-59712-407-2
1. Mumau, Thad. 2. Sportswriters--North Carolina--Biography. 3. Baseball players--North Carolina--Biography. I. Title.
GV742.42.M85A3 2010
070.4'49796--dc22
2010001977

Published by
Parkway Publishers, Inc.
PO Box 3678
Boone, North Carolina 28607
Ph. & Fax: (828) 265-3993
www.parkwaypublishers.com

Contents

For Dahlia
My Love, the best person I have ever known

Introduction

Every year, when the grass turns green, I get this certain feeling. It's a can't-wait, child-like excitement, an anticipation of the near future about to burst forth, spiced with an appreciative gratification for the storied past. I know baseball season is about to begin.

Years ago, Major League Baseball promoted itself with a marvelous slogan — Baseball Fever: Catch It. I think that captures the annual ritualistic feeling I share with millions of baseball lovers.

I use the word lovers because fans, somehow, does not seem strong enough. We baseball lovers are connoisseurs of The Game. It is not simply about rooting for a favorite team or player. That is part of it, but the sheer joy of following baseball collectively is what this feeling entails. It is scouring and devouring box scores, salivating over trade rumors, and secretly predicting which phenoms will blossom into rookie of the year candidates.

When I was about seven years old, my granddaddy and I would sit on the back steps of his house sometimes on summer nights. My granddaddy sat quietly, gazing at the sky, and after a while, he would light up a cigarette. I asked him why he smoked, and he would say, "I don't smoke; I just enjoy a Lucky Strike every now and then. Like when I'm looking up at the stars on a clear night such as this. Or when I'm walking around with Country under the pecan trees late in the evening, just before the sun goes down. Mostly, I like a Lucky when I'm thinking." I would invariably ask, "What are you thinking about?" And, just as invariably, he would answer, "Things."

Country was Granddaddy's old hound dog. That was the nickname of Enos Slaughter, a Hall of Fame outfielder and my granddaddy's favorite baseball player. He loved Slaughter because he was from North Carolina and because he was a hustling ballplayer, but mostly because he scored the winning run in the 1946 World Series for Granddaddy's beloved St. Louis Cardinals.

Occasionally, Country would rise up from the dirt where he was laying, and he would lift his face to the heavens and start to howl. Not hearing another dog off in the distance and not seeing a full moon, which was known to set off the baying of just about any kind of dog, I would ask what Country was going on so about. "Probably nothing he sees or hears," Granddaddy would say, puffing on his Lucky Strike. "I expect he's just barking at memories. We all do that now and then."

Baseball has been a big part of my life for about as long as I can remember. If I wasn't playing it, I was reading about it or listening to games, or watching them when I got the chance. There was always a scuffed-up baseball lying around somewhere in my room, a bat standing in a corner, and a shoebox full of baseball cards sitting on top of my chest of drawers. My walls were plastered with ballplayers' pictures that I had cut out of magazines. Baseball sleeves, a cap, my glove, and an old pair of spikes were usually scattered on the floor.

My name is Thad Mumau, and I am a baseball player. At least, that's the way I like to think of myself. I played baseball on and off for most of my life with varying degrees of success until I ran out of leagues and my legs ran out of steam. Although I was not talented enough to fulfill my big league dream, I'm sure no one had more fun playing baseball than I did.

I haven't played for years now, except in my mind, and I do a lot of that.

Everyone is told not to live in the past, but baseball is a wonderful exception. Reading, learning, and debating about the feats of greats from Babe Ruth to Ken Griffey Junior, from Christy Mathewson to

Greg Maddux ... that is what baseball lovers do. Baseball's past and present, despite their differences, are linked and compared because 90 feet as well as 60 feet, six inches are still the main dimensions on the game's blueprint.

As a sports writer, I never worked in a city where there was a major league team, but I was fortunate to cover Hank Aaron's 715th home run, and along the way, to interview Aaron and fellow Hall of Famers Roberto Clemente, Tom Seaver, Willie Stargell, and Phil Niekro. Other baseball standouts I talked with include Dale Murphy, Dick Groat, Bob Friend, Tony Cloninger, and George Altman.

Among my baseball memories are seeing the M&M Boys play in Yankee Stadium, watching the Braves and Pirates stage their version of home run derby one Saturday afternoon in Atlanta, marveling as Clemente ripped three triples in the same game, and witnessing a terrible collision that could have derailed Milwaukee's 1957 pennant express.

In the pages which follow, I recount these events as I saw them, share what some of the above mentioned players said to me, and also reach back for endearing experiences of my own — among them, getting my first baseball glove, visiting fabled Forbes Field with my daddy, being handed a baggy old uniform by my high school coach, and even making a baseball comeback in my mid-thirties.

These are chapters for baseball lovers and fans, both of whom can identify with the plain-spoken words written in baseball prose and with the emotions evoked by a game that is much more than a game for many of us.

This is the story of me and baseball and barking at memories.

Chapter 1
My First Glove

A tender memory of a little glove and a big heart

I got hooked on baseball at the age of eight. That was when my daddy came home from work one day and handed me a brown paper bag. In it was a baseball glove. It was dark brown with a small web, and it had short, fat fingers and a tiny pocket. It was stubby, not at all like today's gloves which are long and streamlined. The mitt was not one of the name brands found at sporting goods stores. It was a D&M (Draper and Maynard) brand Johnny Sain model, and my daddy bought it at the Western Auto store for eight dollars.

The label meant nothing to me. I thought that glove was beautiful.

It turned out to be the best gift I would ever receive, one which was life-changing. Nothing would provide me as much joy as baseball. And nothing would provide me as much heartache. I loved baseball and everything about it, savoring the nuances which make it so much more than a game.

Daddy taught me how to use the glove, emphasizing that I should catch with two hands if at all possible. He showed me how to squeeze the glove around the ball after it landed in the pocket, how to shift the glove for high and low balls, how to backhand balls to my right. I was fairly coordinated, and snagging the ball in my glove came easily. When an occasional ball tipped off of the glove and popped me in the chin or shoulder, I was more upset about missing the ball than with the sting I felt. My daddy said to throw overhand, because that was the most accurate way and because side-armed throws would often be wild, sailing throws. I was a skinny kid, but I threw a baseball pretty hard and fast.

As time went on, my daddy told me about The Game. For a boy, it was like entering a magic kingdom. I was crazy about baseball, reading books about it, digesting box scores, and daydreaming, always daydreaming. My fantasies featured me in major league games, wearing uniforms that glowed radiantly white, and hitting dramatic ninth-inning home runs, majestic, towering blasts which won games. I wanted to play baseball forever.

I rubbed oil into my glove to soften and treat the leather. My daddy taught me how to do it, to keep the glove from getting too dry without lubricating it too much. I would sit in my room late at night, listening to a Pittsburgh Pirates game on the radio and massaging that leather. I strained to hear Pirates announcer Bob Prince when the static became louder than his distinctive voice. Our house in North Carolina was a long, long way from the KDKA tower, and there were many strong radio signals between us and Pittsburgh. The game faded in and out, from quite clear to nothing at all. My daddy and I would strain to hear whether a Pirate player got a hit or made a catch. I remember sometimes when the Pirates were playing in a big game, Daddy would drive me to the top of a big hill about three miles away. There, with the reception much clearer, we would sit and listen to the last few innings.

I cherished everything about that glove of mine — the smell, the feel, and the transformation that took place whenever I slipped my small left hand inside it. For the longest time, I would put on my pajamas at night and sit on my bed, wearing my Johnny Sain baseball glove. I would hold it over my face, inhaling the intoxicating aromas of baseball. I would lie on my back and toss a ball toward the ceiling, catching it when it dropped lazily back down. There were many nights that I went to sleep hugging that glove to my chest the way lots of kids hold a teddy bear.

My daddy was a tall, slender man who reminded folks of Abraham Lincoln, especially when he grew a beard and wore a top hat for our city's birthday celebration. He was 6-foot-4, but looked taller because of his slim stature, which belied the fact that he was a powerfully strong man.

I bragged to friends that my daddy had been a catcher for the New York Yankees. When my mother heard this story, she scolded me for lying and said I would have to tell my buddies the truth. I rationalized that Daddy was, indeed, a "yankee" — having been raised in the North — and that he had been a catcher for his high school and American Legion baseball teams. Mother smiled, but insisted on me straightening the crooked tale. My friends liked the lie better than the truth. They were disappointed to find they did not know a former big league player personally.

Some things you never forget. Daddy and I had so much fun playing catch, and we always looked forward to the next time. We would spend an hour or more, just throwing the ball back and forth. Sometimes we said nothing; we just smiled at the sweet sound of a baseball smacking into a pocket of leather. He had an old catcher's mitt, saved from his high school days, with the leather worn rough as if it had been scrubbed with sandpaper.

Most summer evenings, if it wasn't raining, I would get that battered mitt, a ball, and my own glove, and I would sit on the little side porch of our house and wait for my daddy to come home from work. When he drove up, I would run to the car and ask him to play catch with me. I was not old enough to think about how tired my daddy might be after working hard for nine or ten hours. And he worked plenty hard, changing tires all day using nothing but an old-fashioned lug wrench, a hydraulic jack, and muscle. But he never complained. He would get out of the car, smile, and say, "Let me put up my lunch pail and get a glass of water, and I'll come right back out." And he always did.

I owned two other gloves before I finished high school, and both were unique. There was a Stan Musial model, a Rawlings three-fingered job which was longer than the glove I had been using, and the added length enabled me to reach some balls that would have eluded me before. My last glove was so large that I felt embarrassed when I missed a ball. It was a six-finger, Roger Maris model Spalding Trapocket, very similar to the Trap-Eze made by Rawlings. Its special feature was a slender finger-shaped piece of leather where the web was normally located, hence the six-finger description. The elongated web area added flexibility, making the glove ideal for the outfield as well as first base. I liked it much better than a first baseman's mitt because the latter always seemed stiff to me and was not nearly as good for fielding ground balls. Compared to my first glove, the Trapocket looked like a bushel basket.

It was my newest treasure, but the old Johnny Sain glove was not forgotten. In fact, it never has been. I still have it, along with the sweet memories. It was my introduction to baseball.

Sport was my favorite magazine when I was growing up. I especially liked it in the summer. The magazine's features on baseball players made me feel as though I knew them, and I cut out the glossy color photographs that accompanied the articles.

My walls were filled with pictures of Ted Williams, Warren Spahn, Roberto Clemente, Willie Mays, Yogi Berra, Hank Aaron, Roy Campanella, Nellie Fox, and many others. My mother was good about letting me put up as many of the pictures as I wanted. She gave me straight pins to use because they did not make big holes as tacks would have and they didn't peel paint off of the walls like tape would have. I read everything about baseball I could find. In fact, most of my book reports for school were about baseball players' biographies or baseball fiction by John R. Tunis and Matt Christopher. I guess you could say I went nuts over baseball.

I noticed everything about major league baseball players — their batting stances, the way some wore long sleeves under their uniform shirts while others had cut-off under sleeves, and the fact that many of them chewed tobacco. Nellie Fox had the biggest chaw I had seen, with every picture of the White Sox second baseman showing him with one jaw protruding almost grotesquely. I had no idea what tobacco tasted like, but I sure wanted to chew some because I thought that was what ball players did.

So, one day, when my mother was gone and my daddy was in the bathroom, I decided to try some tobacco. The trouble was, I didn't know there were different kinds for different uses. Daddy had a tin of Prince Albert pipe tobacco sitting on top of his dresser, and I sneaked it out of the house. I walked to my uncle's nearby field which was grown up with broom straw. It was so high that I was hidden by the yellow-brown shoots.

I kneeled down, opened the tin, and poured some of the tobacco into my hand. Then I put it in my mouth and tried to chew it. The small particles scattered all over the inside of my mouth, some drifting between my gums and cheeks, some sticking to my teeth, and some trickling down my throat. Moments later, I was gagging.

My daddy came out of the house, wondering where I was, and yelling my name. The best I could manage in reply was a grunt and a groan, and fortunately, I was close enough that he heard me. Pushing his way through the tall, yellow broom straw, Daddy found me on the ground, spitting, sputtering, hacking, and heaving as if I was going to throw up.

He asked what was wrong before spotting his pipe tobacco lying beside me. Not seeing a pipe or any sign of smoke or burned tobacco, he realized what I had done. Daddy tried to hold back his laughter, but he couldn't help himself. Pulling me to my feet and helping me walk to the house, he explained that the tobacco in the tin was not the kind to be chewed. He also pointed out that chewing tobacco was likely to make me just as sick, if not sicker.

Some of my cousins talked a lot about hunting. Rabbit hunting mostly. I had one cousin, Richard, whose daddy owned a pen full of beagles. A time or two, when I was at Richard's house, his older brother and his daddy would get those beagles — there must have been a dozen of them — and they would set out into the woods, hunting rabbits. The dogs would be barking, and after a while, I could hear them howling, and Richard said that meant they were on the scent of a rabbit. About three hours later, they would come back, and the dogs would be panting from thirst and exhaustion. My uncle and cousin were dragging as well. I did not see any sign of a rabbit and knew better than to ask if they had.

I always adored beagles. I think it was their long, floppy ears and their sad-looking eyes. Our family had several beagles at one time or other, but none of them were for hunting. They were just pets. Three of them were hit and killed by cars. Daddy said it happened because the dogs would get their noses to the ground, probably smelling rabbits, and the trail would take them across the highway. The one beagle we had that was not hit by a car ran off into the woods one day and never returned. My family figured she met up with someone else who liked beagles.

I never have liked guns. My daddy did not own one as he was neither a hunter nor a shooter. One year, I asked Santa Claus for a BB gun, also known as an air rifle. I asked for one because my cousin, Samuel Guy, was asking for one. He said we would go hunting together. The idea of shooting animals of any kind really didn't appeal to me, but Samuel made it sound like fun.

Sure enough, we both got BB guns for Christmas, and a few days later, Samuel came over to my house, carrying his air rifle. He said we were going bird hunting. We had not been in the woods more than five minutes when we heard birds chirping from branches high above our heads. I did not even see the birds, but I cocked my gun, pointed it among the trees' mass of limbs, and fired. Plop. A cardinal fell right at my feet. There on the ground, not two feet away, lay a cute little red bird, blood spilling from a hole in its chest. I watched as it squirmed around and died. Tears ran down my cheeks. I was distraught.

I emptied all of the BBs from my gun, pouring them onto the dirt, and I ran to our house as fast as I could. I went to our deepest closet, pushed through coats that were hanging and boxes stacked behind the coats, and I shoved my BB gun against the wall. I never touched it again.

It was one more reason to stick with baseball as my favorite sport, hobby, and pastime.

Chapter 2
Cow Pasture Baseball

Playing a great game in a
meager southern setting

    I grew up in the country, just outside the city limits of Fayetteville, North Carolina. It was the country then. Now, what was once farm-land is covered with houses, a large private school, and businesses. There isn't a cow or chicken to be found in a ten-mile radius. There were plenty of both in the mid-1950s. My family lived in a little green-shingled house nestled among pine trees. Our home was down a narrow, two-rutted dirt road on a piece of woods land that was a gift from my mother's parents. They lived up the hill in a white house with a tin roof which played a beautiful symphony when it rained.

Out back was a rickety chicken coop that looked as if it would fall over if a stiff breeze came up, standing shakily behind three towering pecan trees and a maze of grape vines.

I loved spending Saturday mornings with my granddaddy. We gathered eggs in his old felt hat, threw out grain for the chickens, ate mints and cheese biscuits my grandmother made, and played gin rummy and checkers at the dining room table. Sometimes, Granddaddy would toss a baseball back and forth with me, and I was amazed that he caught the ball with his bare hands. Being eight or nine years old, it didn't cross my mind that I did not throw very hard. Because my granddaddy had white hair, I was thinking he was too old to do such a miraculous thing as catch a baseball barehanded.

Back then, the area where we lived was open land and open skies, and there were more animals than people in the countryside which included our narrow little piece of property. On one side of our house was a cow pasture that sloped down from the house and on the other was a corn field that rose over a small hill. Both tracts of land were owned by uncles, brothers of my grandmother. One had a small dairy farm; the other farmed, growing squash, beans, and I don't know what all in addition to corn. Behind our house was a forest thick with pine trees that formed an eternally bright green canopy, with a sprinkling of oak, dogwood, and persimmon.

Tucked among all those trees, about a quarter of a mile downhill, was a small stream that had carved itself a bed into a blanket made by thick layers of leaves accumulated over many, many years. Dark green moss grew nearby in the round shape of a little mound right under a scrub oak. I sat on that soft cushion of moss many a time, tossing pebbles into the water, while daydreaming, thinking, and wondering. The water ran slowly in that little stream, and it made a rippling sound I thought was the most peaceful thing I had ever heard.

One day, after growing older and busier and not visiting the stream for what had been years, I went looking for it. But it was gone, dried up and overtaken by the woods' undergrowth. I missed the peaceful sound and the place that had been so special.

Four cousins and I rounded up as many boys as we could, and we played baseball in that pasture. We fashioned a diamond in the flattest portion of the field. Chunks of old plywood or cloth flour sacks filled with dirt served as the bases. Sandspurs were a problem, and there were times when someone fielded a ground ball, only to drop it with a painful exclamation when pierced by one of those little barbs, and a throw was never made.

I remember one time thinking that I would make our ball field look more professional by putting down base lines. Without asking my mother, I took her flour down to the pasture and proceeded to draw lines from home to first base and home to third base. It was a terrible idea. For one thing, the lines were not even close to being straight, and it looked awful. Worse, though, my mother was upset about her flour being wasted. She explained that we did not have money to throw away, and then she told me that I would pay for the flour from my allowance. I got a quarter every week, so I wouldn't be getting anything for two weeks.

There was a brown and white dog that lived at a little house near the pasture. His name was Zachariah, and he sometimes created problems for our ball playing. Occasionally, he would come down to join us. Zachariah wanted to play, too, and he would crouch, waiting for a ball he could grab. If he got to it before one of us did, he snatched the ball and dashed away, wanting to be chased. It would take a long time for him to get tired or just give up, and the chase often took us far across the pasture from where we were playing. After finally grabbing the ball from the dog, we used dirt and our hands to get rid of all the slobber. When we saw Zachariah trotting down to our game, we knew we were in for some interruptions and a lot of running.

The great thing about cow pasture baseball was that it had no season. When the cows were grazing far from the area where we played, the weather was clear and reasonably warm, and we could gather up at least six boys to play, it was game time. Usually, all but one of the players were cousins. The sixth boy, Shelton, lived about a quarter of a mile away, and he didn't really like baseball. He got a kick out of watching cows being milked, so my three cousins whose family owned the cows would promise Shelton free admission to a milking in return for his making the sides even for our game. If any of us had friends visiting, they played too. The games generally lasted almost all day. They were played on Saturdays or during the summer when

13

school was out.

We started in mid-morning, went to my house for a lunch of bologna sandwiches and Kool-Aid, and played until supper time, which was around six o'clock in the evening. Bathroom breaks were taken behind trees or in the bushes. Since we had a small number of players on each team, we adopted rules to fit the situation. A ball hit to the opposite field — left for a left-handed batter and right for a right-handed batter — was an out. It was also an out if a defensive player threw the ball between the runner and the base to which he was heading.

There was one special ground rule: a ball that landed in a cow paddy was an out, and whoever hit it had to retrieve the ball and clean it. That was done by wiping the ball on grass or weeds, rubbing it in the dirt, and then rubbing it on the grass again. No matter how much dirt we rubbed into our hands after such an ordeal, they still stunk. But smelly odors were simply a hazard of cow pasture baseball.

Our equipment was fairly primitive. When one of us was fortunate enough to get a new — or barely used — baseball, we brought it to the pasture for the game. Most of the time, we used the same old ball over and over. After a while, the stitching of the seams of a ball would break loose, and the cover would come off. We wrapped those balls with black electrical tape, and they lasted a long time. The same kind of tape was used on broken bats, which was about all we ever had. A splintered bat handle would be covered with black tape, sometimes on top of a nail driven into the broken area. Taped balls and bats were the norm.

Pitchers did not throw hard in the pasture. There was no catcher, and the idea was to let the batter hit the ball and hope it was hit at a fielder. Because there were not a lot of fielders, runners circled the bases with great frequency, and scores were high. We always kept score, but did not count innings. Sundown or supper time was the ninth inning. If one team got far ahead, we would start a new game. Those games were great fun, and like the other boys, I fell down laughing when someone hit a ball that landed in cow poop.

I took the games more seriously than the other boys, though, and I would get mad at myself if I missed a ground ball or dropped a fly. It bothered me to make the last out of an inning with runners on base.

And I hated to lose.

Samuel, my best friend growing up in addition to my cousin, lived across the corn field from me. We saw each other almost every day, were in Cub Scouts and Boy Scouts together, attended the same church, and took turns eating meals and spending nights at each other's house. He also liked baseball, and we had great fun throwing catch and hitting fly balls to one another.

There were a lot of times when we could not get up a game, and I couldn't go over to Samuel's house or he couldn't come over to mine, so I used my imagination and came up with a number of games I could play by myself. I plucked red berries off of our shrubbery, tossed them into the air, and hit them with a stick. Depending on where the berries landed, the batter would get a single, double, triple, home run, or an out. Using the lineups of two big league teams and keeping tabs in my head what each hitter did, I played games. My mother stopped that game before our bushes were left naked.

So, I did the same thing with a plastic ball and bat. I had to chase the ball every time I hit it, but I didn't mind. It was a form of baseball, and when I was playing baseball, I never got tired. Time was not a factor because I seldom had somewhere I had to go. Although I spent quite a bit of time by myself, when I was playing my little games, I didn't feel lonely at all. The big league players in my imagination were right there with me.

I also found ways to practice fielding by myself. I threw a rubber ball high into the air so that it would land on the roof of my grandparents' house. The roof was pitched at a severe angle so that the ball would take high bounces back to me, and, depending on what part of the roof the ball had hit, the carom might shoot over my head or drop far in front of me. I had to go back or come in to make the catch. It was a good way to improve my ability to judge fly balls. For grounders, I stood in our front yard and threw the rubber ball hard against the brick chimney. Depending on where I threw the ball, it would bounce straight back to me, or to my left or right, and the closer I stood to the house, the faster my reflexes had to be in order to make the play. That really helped to widen my range and quicken my hands.

Doing those things was fun, but I lived for games in the pasture.

There were times when cows were almost in our yard. They would come up to the barbed wire fence that separated the pasture from our land, and they would just stand there. Cows are such gentle animals, and I sometimes petted them like I would pet a dog. When they were that close to our house, though, I knew there could be no ball game.

If I got up in the morning on a Saturday or during the summer and saw the cows far on the other side of the pasture, I started calling my cousins to see who could play and calling friends who lived fairly close to see if they could come over. I was the game organizer. When I rounded up enough players for a game, I was very excited. Usually, that meant three on each team. Once in a while, we would get six or seven boys on a team, and that was almost like a real game because we could hit to any field. When I tried to arrange a game and it didn't work out because boys couldn't or wouldn't play that day, I was very disappointed.

Those games, with cattle watching from a distance as our spectators, and with sandspurs, cow poop, and a ball-swiping dog as obstacles, were tremendous fun. It was a bit more fun for me because, at the end of the day, I mentally reviewed how I had played and thought about how I hoped to improve. I never could wait for the next game.

It was the first baseball I ever played, and it didn't matter that the balls and bats were taped or that much of our energy was used chasing balls that seemed to roll forever because of the shortage of fielders. When I felt the ball plunk into my glove as I made a catch or I heard and experienced the thwack of my bat making solid contact with a pitch, it was spectacular. Just as good as it ever got.

Chapter 3
Learning About Fairness

A mother dispels the color barrier

Across the cow pasture, on the edge of a wooded area, stood a tiny shack where a black family lived. The boards on the house were gray from years of pounding by the burning sunshine, freezing winds, and pelting rain. The frame structure had never been painted. There was a crooked smokestack on the sagging roof, which was patched all over with tin, hunks of boards, and pieces of mismatched shingles, and an outhouse sat back in the trees. Electricity was not available.

Jeremiah Williams and his wife, Cora, worked on my uncle's dairy farm. They had five children. Jim, the oldest, was ten, eight months older than me.

Sometimes when we played baseball in the pasture, Jim would walk down and get in the game. I remember the first time that happened. He was watching us from the front of his house, sitting on a big log that his daddy would split to burn in the fireplace so the family could cook and stay warm. The Williams' place was maybe 150 yards from where we played our games. Another player was always welcome, so everybody yelled and motioned for Jim to come down. He shook his head and went into the house.

A little while later, he came back out, sat down on the log, and went back to watching us play. Again, we shouted for him to come and play with us. This time, he jumped off of the log and sprinted to where we were. He was grinning broadly. We all introduced ourselves, and he told us his name was James Nathanial Williams but that he went by Jim. He saw that we all had baseball gloves, and he sheepishly said that he could not play because he didn't have one. We told him that when his team was in the field, he could use the glove of one of the players on the team at bat, and he seemed both surprised and happy.

This was the 1950s, and blacks in the South — we called them colored people back then because no one knew any better — did not mix with whites and were thought by society in general to be inferior. I did not understand that. My mother taught me when I was a very young boy to treat everyone like I wanted to be treated. She told me to say yes sir to men and yes ma'am to women and to always hold the door for females. Mother did not differentiate, did not specify that those rules applied only to certain people or to people with light skin.

As I grew up, there were friends and relatives who chastised me at times for following my mother's golden rules. If I said no ma'am to a black woman or held the door for one, these people would say things like, "Why did you say that? Why did you do that? You don't have to." I told them that, yes, I did have to do that because my mother told me people are people and that skin color does not make them different.

Of course, when I looked around, I knew most folks did not think that way and that, in truth, blacks were very different — not in the kinds of people they were, but in the demeaning way they were looked upon and treated. I knew that was not fair, and sometimes it bothered me.

We were playing baseball in the pasture one Saturday, and it got to be close to lunch time. Nobody was wearing a watch; our stomachs told us it was around noon. Mother had told me all of us boys could eat at our house that day; she would fix sandwiches. She could not do that all the time, but she fed everybody when possible.

On this particular day, my mother shouted down to us that lunch was ready. Everyone went except Jim. We did not even notice he wasn't with us until we sat down on the front porch, where Mother had brought the food. Someone mentioned that Jim wasn't there. We looked down to the pasture, and there he was, just sitting on the ground.

Then my mother did the most wonderful thing. I remember she was wearing a skirt and blouse, and she walked over to the barbed wire fence which separated our yard from the cow pasture. She held her skirt with one hand, pushed down the middle strand of wire with one foot, pulled the top strand up with the other hand, and she climbed through the opening into the pasture. She walked down to where Jim was, talked to him a few minutes, and, holding his hand, walked him back to where we were. He ate with us, and when we were finished, Mother said to Jim, "You are welcome at our house anytime." Jim answered that he was not supposed to go into a white family's house. My mother told him she didn't believe that hogwash, adding, "I hope you will come and visit us again."

That is the way my mother was. She showed my sister and me the right things to do because she did them; she lived them. Julia Mae, the black woman who helped my grandmother make cakes for a living, stayed with my sister and me sometimes when our parents were gone. Julia had eleven children and a husband whose visits home were few and far between. Nine months after one of his short stays, another child would be born. Mother said to her one day, "Listen, I know the Lord said to go ye and populate the earth, but Julia Mae, He didn't intend for you to do it by yourself." My mother took Julia to the health department and made arrangements for her to undergo a procedure which would prevent her from having any more children.

One of those eleven children was shot to death by accident. The boy was six years old. After that happened, my mother prepared food and took it to Julia's house. She stayed with Julia's children much of one night and another whole day. She attended the funeral. A woman we knew had the audacity to call Mother on the phone and ask what she thought she was doing, coming out of "that colored neighborhood" late at night. My mother said, "I was visiting one of my best friends", and she slammed the phone down. You had better believe all of that made a lasting impression on me.

One day, during a game of baseball in the cow pasture, I was pitching and Jim was batting. He hit a little roller back to me, and I bobbled it. When I finally picked up the ball, it was too late to get the out. In frustration and anger, I threw to first anyway, and I threw the ball very hard. It sailed to the left of the first baseman and hit Jim on the leg.

He fell to the ground, writhing in pain and holding his leg. I knew he was hurt, and as we all gathered around Jim, I saw this look in his eyes as they spilled over with tears. I was afraid the hurt in his eyes wasn't just from being hit with a baseball. I was afraid Jim might have thought that I hit him just because I could, that with his being the only black boy in the crowd, he had to take whatever we dished out. For some reason, I didn't know how to tell him that wasn't it at all. I didn't know what to say, so I didn't say anything. I went home that night, wondering what I should do.

I kept wondering, and then one day, I learned that Jim and his family were gone. I had waited too long to apologize, to tell him that I didn't mean anything by hitting him, that it was just a wild throw and was done out of anger at myself. I did not think about it all the time, but the incident remained at the back of my mind. I was concerned that it was on Jim's mind, too.

It was six years later before I saw him again. One night, I stopped at an open-air market (what we called convenience stores) to get a cold Pepsi. I went to the big barrel filled with ice and soft drinks, and I reached in to grab a Pepsi-Cola. When I turned to go to the counter and pay, a young black man was standing there. We looked at each other. "Jim? Is that you? Is your name Jim Williams?" He said it was, and I set my drink on the counter and gave him a hug. I don't think he knew what to think. I was overjoyed as I told him my name, then apologized for hitting him with a baseball when we were young boys. Jim said he had forgotten all about that, and that he never thought much about it. He said he just remembered that his leg hurt when the ball hit him and that it left a bruise for a while. He said other than that, he didn't think anything of it.

That was a happy, happy night.

I always hated the word nigger. I have never said the word, and I feel kind of guilty even writing it. Several black people worked for a man who lived on a farm a half mile or so from us. He and his son called them niggers to their faces. Even as a small boy, I bristled when I heard that. Those black people were not slaves, and they were not beaten, but they were not treated like white workers would have been treated.

My mother did not use that word, but my daddy did. He worked with some black men, and a few of them gave him a hard time. As service manager of a tire store, Daddy was responsible for taking old tires off of cars and putting new tires on them. He did much of the work himself. Some of the men who were supposed to help often showed up late for work or just quit in the middle of a sweltering afternoon. Sorry workers — black and white — were fired by my daddy if they didn't quit first. Twice, black men he had fired came back about nightfall with bellies full of wine. They threatened my daddy, and one of the men pulled a knife on him one evening.

Daddy didn't talk about these incidents when I was around, but I overheard stories he shared with Mother. He spoke with disdain and usually connected the term no-good with the word nigger. I cringed each time he used that phrase.

One night at the supper table, I confronted my daddy. I don't know why, because it wasn't planned; I just did it. It was a reaction. I asked him to please stop saying the word — and I spelled it: n-i-g-g-e-r — because his using it made it sound like he was not a nice man. I appealed to his being a baseball fan. I asked if he didn't think Willie Mays and Roberto Clemente were good guys, and would he call them that word. I argued that every colored person was not lazy or mean, and that Mays and Clemente were just two examples. And then I told Daddy that word was shameful, that it was an insult to colored people as well as to himself.

The room grew dreadfully quiet. Daddy didn't say anything; he just stared at me. And he did not look happy. In our home, sassing was forbidden, and I was thinking what I had basically done was sass my daddy. Why had I been so bold, so foolish? I was hoping he would not explode.

He didn't. Instead, after a few pensive moments that seemed like hours to me, Daddy said, "Son, you're right. I never thought of it like that. I was judging every colored person on the few bad ones I had to deal with at work. I will not use that word any more."

I was very proud of my daddy … and very relieved.

Chapter 4
The Golden Fifties

A boy's early introduction to big league baseball

The 1950s were a golden era for baseball, with Willie, Mickey, and the Duke patrolling center field for the three big league teams in New York City, and with Teddy Ballgame and Stan the Man reigning supreme at the plate.

My introduction to major league baseball was in the living room of our house, sitting by the radio with my daddy. We didn't have a den; in fact, I never even heard of a den or a great room for many years. All of the houses I visited just had living rooms. Ours was fairly small, as were the two bedrooms, kitchen, bathroom, and dining room. Designers today would describe our house as cozy. My parents said it was just plain little.

Dad liked to listen to the Pittsburgh Pirates' games on the radio, tuning in to KDKA in Pittsburgh. Our radio was box-like and brown, with kind of a fake wood look. There was a big old dial and knobs, all brass colored. Dad would turn the tuning knob ever so gingerly, trying to land it in just the right place, 1020 AM, so he could hear his Pirates play. Some nights, that just wasn't possible, what with all the interference from stations located closer to our home putting out a stronger signal. But, for some reason, it always seemed that we could get the New York Yankees' game, and it was usually pretty clear.

My daddy did not particularly care for the Yankees. He said they had more money than any of the other teams and that they could buy players at will. That was the mid-1950s, and people have been saying — with considerable accuracy — the same thing ever since. The Yankees always seemed to win; at least, they usually contended for the American League pennant even if they didn't win it. They played in the World Series nine times in a ten-year stretch from 1949-58, winning seven championships during that period. Dad said he would like to see somebody else win for a change. But even if it was the Yankees, it was baseball, so we listened to their games quite a bit.

Yogi Berra was one Yankee player my daddy liked. I mean, really liked. The main reason was that Berra was a catcher, and that was the position Dad had played. He watched catchers very closely — the way they gave a target to pitchers, how they blocked balls in the dirt, and how well they threw to second base. My daddy said Berra was a good defensive catcher, but that he was an outstanding hitter. He also said Yogi was a character who said funny things.

When I began to follow baseball, I pulled for the Milwaukee Braves, largely because of Warren Spahn, whose windup I absolutely adored. I was nearly ten years old when I first started keeping up with baseball statistics, and old Spahnie was a 20-game winner every year there for a while. I liked other Braves players, too. I wished (who didn't?) that I could hit like Hank Aaron and Eddie Mathews, and I got a kick out of the way Joe Adcock feasted on Brooklyn pitching and Bob Buhl tamed Dodger hitters. I thought it was neat how Lew Burdette would fidget around on the mound, get hitters all stirred up about the possibility that he threw a spitter, and then throw big pitches in the clutch.

My favorite uniform was worn by the Cincinnati Redlegs, and I especially liked those white caps with the red bills. One time when I went to a minor league game with my daddy, the manager of our home team gave me a batting helmet which had a crack in it. I took it home and painted the crown white and the bill red. I showed it to my mother, and she said it was pretty, but that I shouldn't have used enamel house paint on a batting helmet.

I also liked the Reds' lineup, which was packed with power — big Ted Kluszewski with those muscles popping out of his cut-off sleeves, Gus Bell, Wally Post, and Frank Robinson, who broke in with 38 home runs as a 1956 rookie. But my favorite Redleg was George Crowe. I think what attracted me to him was that he was a back-up first baseman, and when he got the chance to be a front-line player, he made the most of it. That was 1957, when Crowe filled in for the injured Kluszewski and hit 31 home runs. Crowe, who was the first Indiana Mr. Basketball, became an outstanding pinch hitter and smacked 14 career home runs coming off the bench.

Crowe was involved in one of the most bizarre All-Star games of all time. It occurred in 1957 and was really all about the National League starters and not the game itself. I read about it in the news-paper, and looking back, I suppose it was my first introduction to "politics".

Fans' votes determined the starting eight position players in each league, and Cincinnati fans basically stuffed the ballot box. When votes were counted, all eight National League starters were Redlegs. Baseball Commissioner Ford Frick intervened and named Stan Mu-sial to start at first base in place of Crowe, Willie Mays in center field in place of Bell, and Hank Aaron in right field in place of Post. Catcher Ed Bailey, second baseman Johnny Temple, shortstop Roy McMillan, third baseman Don Hoak, and left fielder Frank Robin-son were the Cincinnati representatives remaining as starters.

The confusion and controversy led to a change in 1958, with play-ers, not fans, voting on the starting eight. That procedure continued until the vote was returned to the fans in 1970.

I thought the White Sox had some of the best names, with Nellie

Fox, Minnie Minoso, and Jungle Jim Rivera. And, then, they were called the Go-Go Sox in 1959 because of the way they built their offense on speed (113 stolen bases, just 97 home runs). In my mind, Rocky Colavito was the perfect baseball name. He had a bit of theatre in him, too, putting the bat behind his back and flexing his muscles before stepping into the batter's box. Hitting 83 home runs over the last two years of the decade didn't hurt, either. And, for pure country color, it is hard to match Willie Jones, the third baseman from North Carolina, the guy they called Puddin' Head.

I liked a bunch of shortstops from the 1950s. Pee Wee Reese because I thought he was small (turned out his nickname had nothing to do with his stature). Roy McMillan because he wore glasses and he was such a slick fielder. Luis Aparicio because of his ability to steal bases. Dick Groat because of the way he executed the hit and run. Alvin Dark for the same reason. Ernie Banks more for his sunny disposition than his prolific home run stroke. Granny Hamner because of his first name.

I was also partial to infielders who were not standouts. Guys like Billy Consolo, Herbie Plews, Ted Kazanski, Rocky Bridges, Alex Grammas, Solly Hemus, Billy Gardner, the Bolling brothers (Milt and Frank), Jerry Lumpe, George Strickland, and Sammy Esposito.

The Pirates had the O'Brien twins, and they were identical in every way. They looked just alike, and both were mediocre ball players. Infielders who also tried pitching, Johnny batted .250 lifetime in 248 games, Eddie .236 in 108 games.

The Pirates were great for novelty, but not much for talent. They were the only team I ever knew of to wear batting helmets all of the time. Pittsburgh wore helmets in the field as well as at bat in the early 1950s. A story went around that the Pirates were ordered by their front office to wear the hard hats on defense because they were so bad and needed the protection. Although the club was, indeed, very bad, that story was not true. I sure remember it, though.

When I was in the third grade, I had to wear this cap to school in the wintertime. My mother made me wear it. I hated that cap. It was what would later have been called dorky-looking, but there was no word to describe how bad it looked to me. It had those fur-lined flaps that pulled down over the ears, with a strap that snapped under the chin. Mother said that wearing it would keep the cold out of my ears while I waited by the road for the school bus. She didn't know I never pulled the flaps down when she wasn't around. I would rather my ears freeze off than to be seen with those stupid-looking flaps wrapped around my head.

One day, on the way home from school, two older boys snatched that cap off my head and started playing keep-away from me. The windows were down on the bus because it was a warm afternoon, and my cap sailed right out of the bus and landed on the road. My first reaction was relief as I was glad to be rid of that old eyesore, but then I thought about my mother. When I got home, she asked right away where was my cap. Had I put it in my book sack? Had I left it at school? I mumbled that it was laying somewhere on Raeford Road, the main highway near our house.

After I repeated the sentence so she could understand it, I added that the cap could probably never be found (although I wondered who in the world would want it). She told me to get in the car, that we were going to look for that cap because she couldn't afford to buy me another one. I said that was okay, that I could do without a winter cap, but she didn't agree.

Unfortunately, that old brown cap was lying in plain sight, right out in the middle of the road. Mother pulled the car over, and I grudgingly walked out and picked up the cap. And I continued to wear it to school. Only, then, it had tire marks on it.

It took a while before our family was able to get a TV. I saw sets in friends' houses, and they told me about watching baseball games on television. So, I was pretty excited when my parents announced we were buying one.

On October 15, 1954, our school closed early and students were sent home in anticipation of some very bad weather. It was a Friday, and it was my sister's second birthday. I remember thinking it was grand that the early dismissal meant the weekend was going to be longer. By the time I stepped off the school bus in front of my grandparents' house, the wind was really whipping up and trees were starting to sway. It was difficult walking down the hill to our house because I felt as if I might get blown away.

Hurricane Hazel was a terror, ripping across eastern North Carolina, flattening the state's beach dwellings, and doing more than 130 million dollars of damage in our state alone. There was a gigantic chinaberry tree growing about fifty feet from our house. Hazel practically uprooted the tree, and fortunately, it fell away from us. If it had gone the other way, our home would have been crushed.

The next day, everybody's television antennae were down. Some were on the ground, bent and twisted, and some were snapped off and laying on roofs. Everyone was calling to have someone come out and repair or replace an antenna. The first house in our area to have one put up was ours. The man from Sears Roebuck came out in his truck bright and early Saturday morning.

When you live in a rural area as we did, any visitor was big news, and everybody knew about it. So, by the end of the day, the grapevine was spreading the question, "Why did the TV man go to the Mumaus' house first?" The answer was simple. Our family had purchased our very first TV set the previous week, and it was sitting in our living room when Hazel hit. We were on the Sears schedule to have an antenna erected on Saturday morning. Until the correct information circulated, there were folks who believed we must have some kind of connection to receive such fast attention hours after a hurricane hit.

Normally, I didn't get to see any World Series games played on weekdays. But on Monday, October 8, 1956, my mother picked me up early at school because I had a dentist's appointment. We went home first so I could brush my teeth, and I turned on the television in hopes of seeing part of the game before we left. It was Game Five, and the Brooklyn Dodgers were playing the New York Yankees.

The game had gone fast. It was a pitcher's duel, Sal Maglie throwing for the Dodgers and Don Larsen for the Yankees. Larsen's name was one I barely knew. I did know he had blown a six-run lead in Game Two, lasting less than two innings. But on this day, he was leading, 2-0, in the top of the ninth. As Carl Furillo led off for Brooklyn, I could tell by the announcers' voices that something special was going on.

Furillo hit a fly ball to right field that Hank Bauer caught, and one of the announcers said something like, "Only two batters. That's all Don Larsen needs. Two more outs." Roy Campanella grounded out to second baseman Billy Martin. "One more," is what I think the announcer said. "Just one more out." Dale Mitchell pinch-hit for Maglie, and when he took a called third strike, the announcer shouted that it was a perfect game.

Don Larsen had pitched the first (and still the only) perfect game in World Series history. Yankees catcher Yogi Berra ran out and jumped into Larsen's arms. It was time for us to leave. I always dreaded trips to the dentist's office, and that day was no different. Except that my mind was occupied with Larsen's perfect game. I remember thinking how fantastic it was that someone so scarcely known could achieve such a feat.

One of my '50s favorites was John "Tito" Francona, the father of Boston Red Sox manager Terry Francona. Tito, playing for the Cleveland Indians, finished the 1959 season with a .363 batting average, the highest in the American League. But he did not win the batting title. He had 399 at-bats, leaving him one short of the total required to qualify for a hitting championship. Detroit's Harvey Kuenn was declared the winner with a .353 average.

Some things just stick in a person's memory. Like Dale Long catching in two games for the Cubs in 1958. He was left-handed, and a southpaw catcher is a rarity. Of course, Long was better known as a power-hitting first baseman who set a major league record (since equaled by Don Mattingly and Ken Griffey Junior) by hitting a home run in eight consecutive games for the 1956 Pirates.

Also from the '58 season came what has become a landmark photo of forty-one-year-old Enos Slaughter trudging off the field with his jersey almost ripped off and his hat on backwards after joining his New York Yankee teammates in a brawl with the Chicago White Sox. It was a grand shot of an old warrior.

I discovered baseball cards, and I was dazzled by the colorful photos adorning the front of the cardboard rectangles. Just as intriguing was the back of the cards, which included player statistics and a trivia cartoon. To me, each card was a work of art. I was entranced by the pictures of players I had heard about on the radio.

Our family did not get a television set until after I was eight years old, and I listened to baseball games on the radio. Many years later, I still preferred hearing games rather than watching them on color TV.

Mutual Broadcasting, with a play-by-play announcer named Van Patrick, aired a Game of the Day each afternoon, and I listened in the summer whenever I could.

I grew familiar with names such as Ted Williams, Stan Musial, Yogi Berra, Mickey Mantle, Willie Mays, Warren Spahn, Henry Aaron, and Robin Roberts. When I fingered cards with their pictures on them, I felt I was holding treasures. Back then, a kid could get a card for a penny. It came in a brightly colored waxed wrapper and included a chunk of horrible bubble gum. The gum was pale pink, hard as a brick, and lost its sweetness in seconds. My friends and I chewed it anyway, but we did not care about the gum. The cards were the prizes.

It was not easy to find places that sold baseball cards. The ones that did might only stock one box at a time, and then, it would be weeks before more came in. When they were available, I did not always have money to spend, and when I had some change, it was enough to just buy a small number of cards. The most I ever had to spend at one time was a dollar.

Because purchasing the cards was not something I could do often, and because cards of the biggest stars were somewhat harder to get, there were players whose cards I did not acquire for years. Stan Musial is the first one to come to mind. And there were other lesser standouts. So, what I did was to cut out pictures of those players from magazines or the newspaper and glue them to pieces of cardboard I had cut out the same size as actual baseball cards. Homemade cards.

Twenty years later, people would use baseball cards as investments, buying up "star" cards and hoarding them. It was a new form of speculating, with collectors waiting for the cards' value to increase and then selling them for large profits. Baseball card price guides were published, and they included monetary values of every card ever printed. There was nothing like that happening when I was a boy.

My friends and I simply loved the cards, and we readily swapped doubles, giving up an extra Mantle for a player we didn't have, even a utility guy like Ted Lepcio or Billy Klaus. Doubles were kept in paper grocery bags, while collections were bunched by teams, held together with rubber bands, and stored in shoe boxes.

Most of us can recall the thrill of opening gifts on Christmas morning when we were small. It was exciting to tear off the pretty paper in anticipation of what was inside. Ripping away those waxed wrappings on baseball cards to find the surprise inside gave me pretty close to the same feeling. I always got a kick out of doing that, and it was even more fun when a bunch of us boys went together to buy cards. We all hoped for a Mantle or Mays or Williams or Aaron, and when one of us lucked up, he would shout, "I got Mickey Mantle!" or "Wow, it's Willie Mays!" The rest of us, although envious, were glad for our fortunate friend.

Every trip to a dime store or corner grocery or whatever place we had learned was selling cards was a treasure hunt. Sometimes we would only have a quarter to spend, and opening twenty-five packs did not take long. But having that many fabulous gifts made for a great day.

Although Bobby Thomson's "Shot Heard 'Round the World" was the most heralded baseball moment of the decade, I did not learn about it until years later. The biggest thrill of the 1950s for me was Eddie Mathews' stab of Moose Skowron's hot grounder to end Game Seven of the 1957 World Series and give my beloved Braves the championship.

Ted Williams, Roberto Clemente, and Warren Spahn were my favorite players from the time I first knew anything about major league baseball. Now, more than fifty years later, they still are.

A lot happened to me and my family during the 1950s. We moved into a house that had been built just for us. My sister, Judy, was born. I started school, and six years later, so did she. I fell in love with baseball and played my first organized ball. Sadly, at the end of the decade, my mother became sick.

Mother had been an outstanding athlete in her youth. One of my uncles told me about her exploits in basketball and on the tennis court and about how fast she could run. I always wished I could have seen her do some of those things, and one day I got the chance.

It was almost dark one evening in early October of 1955. My parents, my sister, and I were standing in the side yard of our house. I was nine years old at the time, and Mother's health was still good. She had picked my daddy up at work, and the four of us had just stepped out of our car. We saw dust flying from our dirt road, and in the cloud rising out of the two narrow ruts was a black convertible. My daddy said it was a Ford Thunderbird. He said the man driving it was named Flint Collins. I recalled the name and that Daddy suspected the "Flint" was self-anointed because it sounded flashy. My daddy was in the same division with Mr. Collins during World War II, and he said the man was always bragging about something. Dad was surprised by the visit.

Mr. Collins pulled up behind our car, his left arm hanging out of his Thunderbird. He was wearing sunglasses even though the sun had dropped behind the tops of the trees almost a half-hour earlier. His too-black hair was slicked back on the sides like a rock and roll singer, and his white dress shirt was unbuttoned a good way down the front. He jumped out his car, grabbed my daddy's hand and pumped it, and he put out his arms to give my mother a hug. She took a step back and extended her right arm, opting for a handshake instead. She had met Mr. Collins before, and she had said he was too big for his britches. I was not sure what she meant until I met him.

I didn't like him, either, especially after he made a smart-alecky remark about what my daddy did for a living and the "square" car he drove. Nobody talked much except Mr. Collins as he bragged about first one thing and then another. Somewhere in all of his jabbering, he mentioned that he had always been the fastest runner in his crowd, whether at school or in his Army unit. He said he had been approached by a pro baseball team and a pro football team, but that he was making so much money in big business that he didn't have time for games anymore. He said he was heading to Florida on a business trip and just thought he would look up my daddy.

I looked over at Mother, and I could see she had heard enough from Mr. Collins. My parents did not like braggarts. They always told me that if a person had to boast about what he did, then he probably had not done much. They also said that a person's deeds spoke louder than his words. I was six when they told me those things, and I understood. Anyway, all of a sudden, my mother said, "Flint, if you are so fast, why don't you race me?" Mr. Collins looked at her and laughed, saying, "Pat, you are quite the joker, aren't you?" She insisted that she was not kidding, that she wanted to see just how fast he was.

Mr. Collins thought the whole situation was funny, and he was real cocky as he pointed out that he was wearing dress shoes but that it would not matter. Mother took off the high heels she had worn to work. She was wearing a blue dress and nylon hose, and she pulled her long brown hair back and clipped it behind her head. She pointed to a utility pole about 100 yards up the dirt road, said the two of them would start from there, and she drew a line in the sand in front of the grass where our yard began. That was to be the finish line. Mr. Collins walked away with a swagger, his head shaking from side to side like the whole incident was the silliest thing he had ever experienced. Daddy yelled "Go", and Mother and Mr. Collins took off. The skirt of her dress was flying up, and so was the dust, with Mr. Collins left behind from the start. Mother smoked him. I was clapping my hands, and my little sister did the same because she saw me do it. Daddy grinned.

Seeing he was beaten, Mr. Collins stopped running about twenty yards from the finish line, grabbing his leg and starting to limp. "Darn leg," he said, " … old war injury. I sure wish I could have run like I used to. It wouldn't even have been a race." "Yeah, too bad," Mother said. "I sure wish you could have given me some competition."

With that, Mr. Collins suddenly looked at his watch, said he would liked to have stayed, but that he had somewhere he had to be. And he took off, zooming up the dirt road faster than he had come down it. Daddy put his arm around Mother's shoulders and said, "You know, I don't remember Flint getting injured overseas. That sure was great, Pat. That was just great."

I thought it was, too.

Chapter 5
Fun at Forbes

Father and young son visit the Pirates' hallowed grounds

In the 1940s and '50s, the little Pennsylvania town of Indiana was known as the Christmas tree capital of the world. It is better known for being the home of Jimmy Stewart. His father had a hardware store there, and that store is now a museum honoring the Academy Award-winning actor.

Located fifty-five miles northeast of Pittsburgh, in the foothills of the Allegheny Mountains, Indiana was a blue-collar town. It was the home of my daddy, Bill Mumau, whose uncles worked in coal mines and whose father died young after getting tangled in a tire-making machine. Daddy had to learn to walk again after a battle with polio when he was six years old.

Following high school, he drove a truck for a while, then joined the Army and spent all of World War II — from start to finish — in Europe. While in basic training at Fort Bragg, North Carolina, he met a woman, Pat Graham, who worked for the railroad, shipping troops into and out of the Army base. After the war, they married and lived in Indiana. That's where I was born. Pennsylvania was much too cold for a Southern belle, and her husband, who grew up enduring freezing, snowy winters, decided it was too cold for him as well. When I was three years old, we moved to Mother's home town of Fayetteville, which is Fort Bragg's next-door neighbor.

Most summers, until I was thirteen, my daddy's vacation week was used to visit his relatives in Pennsylvania. We would leave at three or four o'clock in the morning, and Daddy would drive the whole way to the house where he grew up on Maple Street in Indiana. His mother lived there along with my daddy's sister and her family. The highlight of that trip, at least for the last three years, was when Dad took me to Pittsburgh to see a baseball game. The Pirates played in Forbes Field, an old stadium with loads of tradition and memories. And there was a special memory for me from all three games we saw at that historic old ball yard.

I was ten years old when my daddy took me to my first major league ball game. The Milwaukee Braves were the visiting team. Dad bought our tickets in the afternoon, hours before game time. As we started walking back to the car, a man standing at a stadium gate asked if we would like to go in and watch batting practice. The Pirates were hitting early, before the gates opened, and the man said nobody was supposed to be inside yet, but he would let us go ahead and enter.

We walked in, and I gasped when I saw that beautiful baseball field. I had never seen so much grass that was so thick and green. The outfield fences seemed so tall and so far from home plate; I couldn't imagine anyone hitting a ball over them. The infield dirt was the color of cinnamon and was as smooth as velvet. The Pirates were taking batting practice, and every time one of them hit the ball, there was a solid THWACK which echoed all over the ball park. The sound was so loud and reverberating, not at all like the one made when my friends and I hit a ball.

We headed down to get as close as we could, and there, right in front of us, were the Braves' players. I recognized a few of their faces from pictures I had seen in magazines. I remember feeling somehow surprised at seeing those men in shirts and slacks, not in baseball uniforms. They looked like everyday people, dressed in street clothes, sitting in the stands, and razzing the Pittsburgh players. My daddy pointed to a bald-headed man, said his name was Warren Spahn and that I should to go speak to him. I was shy and said I didn't want to, but after my daddy kept telling me I should, I bashfully approached the man and said, "Hi ya, Mr. Spahn." He said, "Hello there, kid." And he tousled my hair.

That night, I got the chance to see Spahn pitch. I also saw the magnificent Roberto Clemente in action. It was 1956, his second season in the big leagues.

Back then, teams took infield and outfield practice before games. A coach would hit balls to the infielders and outfielders, and they would practice catching and throwing. It was a chance for second basemen and shortstops to demonstrate how well they could turn double plays. And it was a chance for outfielders to show off their arms.

I was wowed by how high into the air the Braves' and Pirates' coaches hit fungoes. It seemed the balls soared far above the top of the stadium. I was impressed by how easily infielders scooped up hard-hit grounders and zipped the ball to first base with what appeared to be effortless tosses. Outfielders tracked down long drives that looked uncatchable, settling under the descending spheres and making the catches look easy.

When flies were hit to Clemente in right field, I noticed he made many of the catches around his waist, with his glove turned up. My daddy said that was called a basket catch and that it was a trademark of Willie Mays. Although I was very young and knew nothing of the nuances of baseball, I perceived a certain air about this man with the number 21 on his back. He was not yet a well-known player, nowhere near star status at that time, but he was somehow majestic in his movements. He held his head high and carried himself with pride. After watching him for just a few minutes, I said to my daddy, "That Mr. Clemente is something, isn't he?"

He made a throw to second base, then third. Then he went back on a fly ball, came in to catch it on the move, and uncorked a missile to home plate. The throw was made from fairly deep right field, and it traveled on a low line to the plate with the speed of a rocket. The catcher caught the throw right on the plate. I can still remember Dad saying, "Now, that man has an arm on him."

Over the years, that arm would become Clemente's business card. In eighteen big league seasons, he threw out 140 runners from the outfield, leading the National League in assists five times. The assist total would have been much larger except for the fact that base coaches and base runners grew leery and weary of testing the Schenley Shotgun. They decided it was not worth the risk.

Anyone attending a major league baseball game these days will not be treated to the teams taking infield. I think that is a real shame. You can watch batting practice, and while that is fun, one can only see so many bombs land in the bleacher seats before it grows a bit monotonous. Watching professionals flash their leather and arms is something a person who appreciates baseball never grows tired of.

Witnessing Clemente shoot laser beams was pure entertainment.

The game started, and my daddy was cheering hard for the Pirates. But he said he didn't think their chances were good because, first, they were a lousy team, and second, Warren Spahn was pitching for the Braves. Vernon Law was the Pittsburgh pitcher, and he kept Milwaukee from scoring in the first inning.

I thought I was pulling for the Pirates along with my daddy, and then I saw Spahn. When he walked out to the mound and started his warm-ups, my eyes grew wide as I stared at this graceful left-handed pitcher. His windup was beautiful. Holding the ball in his left hand, Spahn would swing both arms back, while toeing the rubber with his left foot, and he stepped back a little with his right foot. He looked like an eagle about to take flight. Then, as he brought the ball into his glove around his belt, he pivoted and kicked his right leg high into air. At the same time, he tilted his body backward and dropped his left arm back, too. When he threw his right leg toward the plate, his left arm moved forward, and then everything fell together — right foot hitting the dirt in the front of the mound just as his left arm propelled the baseball toward home plate.

I was too young and not baseball-wise enough to understand the mechanics of pitching, but I loved that windup. As a result, Warren Spahn became my favorite baseball player, along with Roberto Clemente. As the game progressed, I came to admire the way Hank Aaron swung the bat, and he was also a fine outfielder. I had a special feeling for Clemente, but the fact that the Braves had both Spahn and Aaron caused me to switch favorite teams. Right then and there, I started pulling for Milwaukee to beat Pittsburgh. My daddy couldn't believe it.

And he gave me some good-natured ribbing when the Pirates won the game, 4-3. He asked me did I want to switch back to Pittsburgh. I said no, that I was a Braves fan and would remain one. Pittsburgh led, 2-1, before Milwaukee rallied for two runs in the top of the ninth inning. The Pirates rallied for two of their own in the bottom of the ninth to win. Spahn was the losing pitcher, dropping his record to 10-9. He would finish the season strong, winning ten of his last twelve decisions to end with a 20-11 record. Law pitched a complete game, surrendering a home run to Eddie Mathews in the second inning, to lift his record to 4-12.

Clemente had a single in three at-bats and drove in a run. He was also walked intentionally. In right field, he was as graceful as a swan, gliding under three fly balls and catching them all easily. He also launched one of his powerful throws home to hold a runner at third base. I wished I could move, throw, hit the ball, and run like him.

The next year, we saw the Braves play again. It was July 11, 1957, two days after my eleventh birthday. Milwaukee was on its way to the National League pennant and an eventual World Series triumph over the Yankees. We had really good seats, between home plate and first base, about ten rows back.

In the bottom of the first inning, Pittsburgh leadoff batter Bill Virdon lifted a high pop-up into shallow center field. Milwaukee shortstop Felix Mantilla went out, center fielder Billy Bruton came running in, and they collided. Hard. We could hear the sound of the impact. Both players lay on the ground for a long time, and finally, two Braves helped Mantilla hobble off the field, while Bruton was carried off on a stretcher. Mantilla was out for a while before coming back to finish the season. Bruton did not play again until the next year. Johnny Logan replaced Mantilla at shortstop and hit a home run to help the Braves win, 7-2. I had a wonderful time, but I kept thinking of Mantilla with blood on his face and Bruton as he lay motionless on that stretcher.

In 1958, we saw the Cincinnati Reds play the Pirates. And we watched Roberto Clemente equal a major league record by hitting three triples in the same game.

Facing Reds right-hander Tom Acker, Clemente grounded out to third base in the first inning. Leading off the fourth for Pittsburgh, he boomed a triple to center field, but was left stranded. In the fifth, after two were out, Pirate catcher Bill Hall doubled and scored on a single by pitcher Curt Raydon. Bill Virdon, the Pittsburgh center fielder, doubled Raydon home, and Virdon came around to score when Clemente blasted a drive to right-center field. He tried to stretch the hit into an inside-the-park home run, but was out at the plate on a nice relay from Cincinnati right fielder Jerry Lynch to second baseman Johnny Temple. Temple fired home, where catcher Smoky Burgess made the tag on Clemente. Burgess would later be traded to Pittsburgh and be one of Clemente's teammates during the Pirates' World Championship season of 1960. Clemente's two-out triple in the eighth inning came off Reds right-handed reliever Willard Schmidt. Dick Stuart followed with an RBI single.

The Pirates won, 4-1. It was years later when I found out Clemente had tied a record.

I witnessed some memorable baseball events, but over the years, what has grown to be the most special recollection is of a small boy and his daddy attending big league baseball games together.

I remember thinking back then that I had the best daddy in the world. That feeling has never changed.

Chapter 6
A Suit and a Seat

Earning a "real" spot on a
Little League team

As winter turned to spring in the year 1955, my parents started talking at the supper table about something called Little League. They talked to each other, while I listened, describing how small boys were divided into teams, given baseball uniforms, and then played in games with real umpires and rules. Eventually, they asked me if that sounded like fun. My first response was that it sounded like great fun. So, my mother said she would make a phone call and find out what would be involved for me to play Little League baseball in the summertime.

At first, I was thrilled. Then, when I went to my room and thought about it, I was scared to death. Sure, I could throw and catch the ball with my friends, and I could really smack the soft pitches tossed in the games down in the pasture. But I had never played real baseball. I had never faced a pitcher throwing the ball hard. The Little League ballpark was in the city, and we lived in the country with cows, corn, and broom straw. I was not so sure I wanted to play in the Little League.

I invented all kinds of excuses for not trying out for a Little League baseball team. At the root of them all was anxiety — over not being as good a player as the other boys and thereby feeling humiliated; about fast pitching and possibly getting hit with a hard speedball; and over the possibility that I might not be picked, might not even be placed on a team. I tried convincing my parents that playing in the city would be too much trouble for them, having to drive me to and from practices (if I was lucky enough to make a team, I thought). I reasoned that going down to the cow pasture and playing with my cousins was good enough for me. After all, baseball was baseball.

Mother and Daddy said they understood my hesitancy to try something new, and they didn't insist on my playing organized ball. They did encourage me, saying that while there would be boys who could play better than me, there would also be some who were not as good. My daddy told me that I could field and throw well, and that I could learn to hit. That made me feel better.

But when the big day came, and we arrived at the place where tryouts would be held, I grew frightened and shy again. My mother had to practically push me out of our Chevy station wagon. Walking onto that baseball field was the hardest thing I had ever done. I looked out and saw so many boys much larger than I was, and many of them seemed to catch and throw balls as if it were nothing. There must have been over a hundred of them out there. Numbers were pinned to the back of each boy's shirt, and four men were introduced as the league's coaches. They all carried clipboards or notepads.

Every boy had the chance to field three ground balls and two flies as well as make throws from the shortstop area to first base and from center field to home plate. I bobbled one of my grounders, but kept it in front of me; I caught both flies; and my throws were all strong and accurate. Everyone got four swings at softly tossed pitches, and I hit all four, but only one left the infield and then just barely. I felt I fared better overall than most of the boys, but I still had my doubts as the coaches trooped inside the recreation center to make their picks.

Back then, Little League was for boys between the ages of eight and twelve. It wasn't like today, with T-ball for smaller kids, then coach-pitch, and machine-pitch, those leagues leading up to Little League, which is now for players eleven to thirteen years old. Coaches were allotted a certain number of points which they used to bid on players. Less than half of the boys trying out would be picked. My playing age was nine, though I was eight years old, because my birthday came during the season.

It seemed like forever before the coaches emerged from the building and announced the boys they had chosen. When I heard my name called, I was beside myself with excitement. My team was Moose Lodge. My coach was Henry Goff. In his brief introduction to his new players, it was obvious the man was a piece of work.

Mr. Goff was forty-three years of age and didn't look a day under sixty. He had probably always looked old. He walked gingerly, as if his little bantam-rooster legs were about to snap, he was stoop-shouldered, and his face was a road map of wrinkles. He appeared too ancient and too scrawny to pick up a ball and bat. But, to show how "easy" it was to hit, Mr. Goff would pepper line drives all over the park off our team's fastest pitcher, and he would do it batting one-handed.

He wore a sweat-stained purplish ball cap that had once been navy blue. It was pulled down to just above his eyebrows, its bill bent and twisted, with the fabric shredding. He came to baseball practice every day directly from his job, wearing scraped-up work shoes and khaki-colored shirt and pants that were rimmed with perspiration lines left from hours of lifting in a warehouse. A pencil-thin mustache grew just above his upper lip, and skin hung loosely from his cheekbones, giving his face a hollow, sad expression.

When Henry Goff stepped onto a baseball diamond, he was transformed from eight-to-five laborer into coach extraordinaire. The man was a Little League legend, his teams winning local championships almost every year. He was crusty, loud, proud, and occasionally foul-mouthed. Parents, mostly those from opposing teams, charged that he cussed too much and made winning too high a priority. But the boys who played for Mr. Goff loved him. He promised he would teach us to play baseball the right way.

And he did. Mr. Goff cared about us, but he did not baby us. One day, he was showing outfielders how to drop down onto one knee on base hits to the outfield. The purpose was to prevent the ball from going through players' legs for extra bases. The coach was hitting us hard ground balls, and the third or fourth one hit to me took a bad bounce and popped me in the mouth. I reached up to my lips, and when I brought my hand away, I saw blood. It was the blood more than the pain that caused the tears, but before I could panic, I heard that gravelly voice. Mr. Goff yelled, "Here comes another one, son. You did a good job. That bad hop there is the very reason you are supposed to get down on one knee. Now, do it again." I was so proud that I forgot about my split lip.

After six practices, all in one week, our coach announced who would be getting uniforms. He had explained that there were twenty-two new players, eleven more returning from the previous year's Moose Lodge team, and there were only sixteen uniforms. I was good enough at math to know I was not likely to be wearing one of them, not that summer anyway.

I was right. I was not one of the five new additions, although I would remain part of the team. I would continue to practice with Moose Lodge, and I would sit with the team at games. Just not on the bench because there was not enough room. I sat at the end of the bench, on the ground. That was fine with me. Deep down, I was relieved that I did not have to face those fast pitchers.

More than half of the boys who did not receive a uniform quit. I was happy just to be a part of the team, and I absolutely loved practices. Everything but hitting, that is. I could not wait for fielding practice — catching ground balls and flies and throwing — but I hated batting. It wasn't fun. It was frightening. Mr. Goff pointed out that the speed of the pitch should not bother me, that the pitcher was supplying the power and all I needed to do was make contact. Heck, I couldn't even make myself swing. I was too afraid.

I batted left-handed. I don't know why; it just felt right. I threw right-handed, but batting from the right side was uncomfortable. Later on, batting lefty would prove an advantage since most pitchers were right-handed, and their curveballs would break into me rather than away from me. At the age of nine, I just liked batting left-handed because Ted Williams and Stan Musial did. I mimicked Stan the Man's corkscrew batting stance because it was unusual and "really neat". It worked fine down in the pasture. Not against real pitching, though. I couldn't get uncoiled before the ball was in the catcher's mitt.

My second year, I got a suit and a seat. I was given a white jersey with Moose Lodge printed on the front and the number 48 on the back. The letters and numerals were navy blue, as were the baseball stirrups I received. We had to get our own navy cap. I sat near the end of the bench, getting into a handful of games in the late innings and even starting twice in left field.

I was a full-time starter as an eleven-year-old, playing left field and center, and even moving to second base and first base for the last half of a couple of games. I started and played first base in every game of my final season.

I was a good bunter. That was strangely surprising in a way because to bunt well, a batter must turn around and face the pitcher straight-on, squaring off (moving the top hand up the barrel of the bat to the trademark area) and laying the fat part of the bat on the ball. The idea is to "catch" the ball with the bat, thereby deadening the ball so it does not travel very far. I could always do that well. I was a very good fielder. I usually held onto anything I could get my glove on. My range wasn't terrific, but I learned to get a good jump on the ball in the outfield and to be up on my toes in the infield so I could move quickly toward grounders. I excelled at first base, digging low throws out of the dirt and using my long legs to stretch and make the difference on close plays. I learned to shift my feet around the bag to pluck throws far to my left and right, and I scooped up hard-hit grounders with ease. I liked playing defense.

There is some irony here because, while I was scared to death of getting hit with a pitch, I almost never shied away from a ground ball. No matter how hard it was hit, I always got in front of the ball. I was fearless with a glove on my hand and just as helpless when holding a bat. When the pitcher wound up, it was all I could do to keep from moving away from the plate. I tried desperately to hang in there, to be like most of the other boys who thought about hitting and not about being hit, who never danced around in the batter's box, and who took hard cuts. My mind wanted to stand in and hit, but my feet had other ideas.

I was hit by a pitch twice, both times by the same pitcher in the same game during my last Little League season. I took a fastball in the thigh from a hard-throwing left-hander my first at-bat that day, then was drilled in the head. That, too, was a fastball. I froze on the pitch. I saw it all the way, but I was unable to either duck or pull away from the ball.

Little League batters did not wear helmets back then. We wore ear flaps. They were two pieces of plastic, connected across the top of the head by elastic bands, each piece covering the ear and temple area. They did not provide much protection. When the ball hit me on the flap, there was a sound not too unlike that made by a bat striking a ball. My mother had her head turned, talking to someone, and did not see the ball hit me. When she heard the sound, she thought I had hit the ball, and she shouted with excitement. After all, I did not make contact that often.

Mr. Goff took me out of the game as a precaution, and I was fine. The next day at practice, sporting a small knot on the right side of my head, I anticipated being pampered. Surely my coach would feel badly about my having been hit, not once but twice. I envisioned lollypop tosses from him when it was my turn to bat. I should have known better.

When it came time for batting practice, Mr. Goff called out my name to be first. I had no more than settled into the batter's box when the ball whizzed over my head. His next pitch forced me to hit the dirt, and the third one made me dance out of the way. He fired three more balls directly at me. I dodged all of them.

"See there," he shouted. "You can get out of the way of the ball. Yesterday was just one of those things. Now get in there, forget about getting hit, and hit the baseball." It seemed tough at the time, but I knew it was the best thing my coach could have done. He made me realize that my reflexes would prevent beanings from becoming a regular occurrence. That realization helped diminish my fear, but it could not make me pull the trigger and become an actual hitter.

I was aggressive and eager to swing the bat — when I was riding in the car with my daddy to practices and games. And on the way home afterward, too. But on the field, it was always the same old story. I walked up to the plate, and I stiffened with fright. I had the reputation of possessing a keen eye, and some of the parents said I never swung at bad pitches. The truth was that I seldom swung at any kind of pitch. Since most eleven- and twelve-year-old pitchers were on the wild side, the odds of drawing bases on balls were in my favor. And I did get my share of walks.

My most vivid Little League memories do not involve me. That first season, the one when I was not on the "active roster", we had a star pitcher named Raymond Floyd. Yes, the same Raymond Floyd who became a professional golfing great and won four majors, including a Masters. He was practically unhittable. Raymond continued to show baseball promise, and he always loved the game. Later, during his early years on the PGA Tour, he would spend some time at several spring trainings, working out with the Chicago Cubs.

There was a little guy on the C&I Bank team, and he could hit like nobody's business. Chris Cammack was his name. A preacher's son, he was three years younger than me and several inches shorter. But he hit the ball as hard and as consistently as anybody. He would go on to be voted the Atlantic Coast Conference Player of the Year and earn all-conference honors all four of his seasons as the North Carolina State University third baseman.

And then there were the Wilson Twins. Gary and Jerry, who were a year older than me, also played for C&I Bank. They were identical in appearance and ability. One would pitch, the other would catch, and on the rare days when Jerry or Gary might experience a bit of trouble on the mound, their coach would have them switch places, and the trouble would end. They could both hit, too; it seemed like they got a base hit every time up, and they slugged quite a few home runs. The Wilson Twins were remarkable and locally famous. They were Little League legends in our city. If I fouled a pitch off of either of them, I felt I had a big day at the plate.

Moose Lodge won three league championships in the four years I was on the team. I knew those two things had little to do with one another, though I did contribute to some wins with my glove. As a Little League hitter, I was a major league flop. I should say as a batter because I was certainly no hitter. While other kids were batting in the .400s and higher, I compiled a career Little League average of .242 with no extra-base hits and six RBI (five came on bases-loaded walks). Most of my hits did not leave the infield, and more than half of them were bunts.

I improved every season, I became an outstanding fielder who could play anywhere in the infield and outfield, I learned how to play baseball the right way, and I had a good time. I received a firm foundation which would help me blossom into a pretty good player down the road. But in terms of individual accomplishments, my Little League career was mostly forgettable.

Chapter 7
The Sometimes Super Sixties

Dramatic opening, amazin' ending

Baseball flashbacks of the 1960s are filled with unforgettable images. Carl Yastrzemski plays a drive off of the Green Monster perfectly, Sandy Koufax delivers another unhittable pitch, and Brooks Robinson makes a backhand stab behind third base. There is electricity in Roberto Clemente unleashing one of his clothesline throws, Hank Aaron flicking his famous wrists to send a blast over the fence, Maury Wills swiping one more base, Bob Gibson defiantly daring a batter to dig in, and Willie Mays making a basket catch look elementary.

Baseball in the 1960s was colossal. At least, it was to me. Maybe it was because that was when I kept up with all of the major league teams and players, day to day during the season and even during the winter. That began late in the previous decade when I was able to see box scores on a daily basis and when I discovered *The Sporting News*.

My mother was the one who found that wonderful baseball treasure chest. One day when she was in a drugstore, Mother saw *The Sporting News*, known as the "bible" of baseball. She paid a quarter for a copy and surprised me with it. I eagerly dove into the tabloid-like magazine packed with page after page of baseball news — nothing but baseball at that time. I was delighted to learn that a new issue came out every week, and although I was not getting an allowance at the time, I negotiated for one. I asked for a quarter a week in return for chores I was already expected to do. Mother agreed, mailed a check for the annual subscription cost of ten dollars, and explained to me that I would be required to repay the cost of the magazine. I got a lesson in finances and a huge weekly helping of baseball information in the bargain.

For a long time, our newspaper did not carry major league box scores. When it began to do that, I was so excited. From the start of the season in April all the way through the end of the World Series in October, I read every box score every day. Notice I use the word "read" because that is what I did. I didn't simply scan the boxes, looking for home runs and winning pitchers; I went down every line for every team and all the other stuff too, even including the time it took to play each game.

Much of the gold dripped into the 1960s, which will be remembered as a bridge from the way baseball had been for many, many years to the way it is today. It was a decade of change.

When it began, there were sixteen major league teams comprising two leagues, and the team with the best record from each league met in the World Series. By the time the 1960s ended, there were twenty-four teams, and the leagues had been split into divisions. Playoffs preceded the Series.

A pair of monumental home runs ushered in the 1960s, and both were the things dreams are made of. Bill Mazeroski's seventh-game blast — it would be called a "walk-off" today — was the first to end a World Series, giving the Pittsburgh Pirates victory over the New York Yankees. The second dramatic home run was hit by Ted Williams in his last major league at-bat, a sign-off signature from the game's best pure hitter of all time. Both homers were hit in 1960.

Old stadiums with personality crumbled during the 1960s, and so did the New York Yankees' dynasty. New stadiums popped out rapidly in cookie-cutter fashion, and artificial turf prompted a style of baseball predicated on speed instead of power. Pitching gained prominence as the strike zone was expanded, then lost ground to hitters when the mound was lowered.

The 1960s featured back-to-back Triple Crown winners, the last pitcher to win thirty games in a single season, and a New York Yankee outfielder not named Mantle who broke the mighty Babe's record of slamming sixty home runs in a season.

Williams was the first of fifteen Hall of Fame players to leave baseball during the decade. Stan Musial's last season was 1963. The left-handed hitter with the wacky stance and silky-smooth swing was the National League's answer to Williams in consistency and hitting prowess. Mickey Mantle's final time at bat came at Fenway Park in 1968 — eight years to the day and in the same place that Williams had homered in his farewell trip to the plate.

The decade showcased new stars, including a hit machine called Charlie Hustle, the best all-around catcher the majors have known, and an ex-Globetrotter pitcher who competed as hard as he threw.

There are fond memories of the 1960 season. My daddy's beloved Pittsburgh Pirates were in a pennant race after so many years as the doormat of the National League. Actually, they had been a contender two years earlier and finished second in the standings behind the Milwaukee Braves. In 1960, the Pirates led the league most of the season. Dad was loving it. Although I had been a rabid Braves fan, I cheered along with my daddy that season because I was happy for him and because I was a huge fan of Roberto Clemente, Pittsburgh's talented right fielder.

Dad would come to my room just about every night after we had washed and dried the supper dishes together, and we listened to the

Pirates' games on the radio. Many a night, when the Pirates were in a tight spot, my daddy would sit on the edge of my bed, his elbows on his knees, and his chin cupped in his hands. I sat in the chair at the table where I did homework and listened as he encouraged his team, saying over and over, "C'mon Bucs. You can do it. C'mon Bucs." I smiled silently, enjoying Dad's involvement in the games as much as I enjoyed the games themselves.

We cheered for the Pirates from April through September. Sometimes I would pop corn, and we would eat it along with a cold Pepsi Cola, while listening to Clemente, Dick Groat, Bob Skinner, Don Hoak, and Smoky Burgess come through with clutch hits. We heard announcers Bob Prince and Jim Woods talk about Vernon Law, Bob Friend, and Elroy Face as they mowed down the opposition and loved the way they described Bill Mazeroski deftly turn another double play. We were stunned, almost in disbelief, when Pittsburgh headed into the World Series to play the juggernaut New York Yankees in October.

In those days, all of the Series games were played during the daytime. The weekday games would be over by the time I got home from school. A few teachers, either because they were baseball fans or because they were glad for an excuse not to teach that day, would allow students to listen to the World Series on a transistor radio someone had brought from home. Just about everybody I talked to at school was pulling for the Yankees. They had all heard of Mickey Mantle, Yogi Berra, and Whitey Ford. There weren't many kids who could name a single player on the Pirates. On the day of Game One of the Series, I was saying that I thought Pittsburgh could beat the Yankees. This guy, a classmate, said, "Well, I'll bet you a dollar they can't." Not wanting to back down, I said, "You've got yourself a bet."

I didn't even have a dollar and didn't know where I would get one if the Yankees won the World Series. As a result, I sweated through game after game. My wager drained some of the fun. When the Pirates won the close ones, I breathed a little easier. When the Yankees clobbered Pittsburgh, I felt tense. When Maz smacked his dramatic seventh-game, ninth-inning home run to give the Pirates the championship, I was very happy, excited, and relieved. I collected my dollar and vowed never to gamble again.

Prior to the 1969 season, New York Mets first baseman Ed Kranepool was asked what he thought of his team's chances to win the National League pennant. "As much of a chance as there is of putting a man on the moon," Kranepool answered. The United States did put a man on the moon — just three months later — and the Mets did win the pennant. They stormed back from a ten-game deficit in early August, winning twenty-four of their last thirty-two games. Tom Seaver won ten straight decisions down the stretch to earn the Cy Young Award with a 25-7 record, a 2.21 earned run average, and 283 strikeouts in 290.2 innings. The Mets completed their "amazin'" season by beating Baltimore in the World Series.

Mother's feet started hurting around 1956. The pain continued, and doctors could not find a reason for it. She went to prestigious hospitals and saw noted specialists all over the country. My daddy took her to Duke Hospital, Memorial Hospital in Chapel Hill, the Cleveland Clinic, and to Methodist Hospital in Houston. The doctors at those places had never seen another case like hers. They said my mother's blood vessels were the size of an infant's; they had not grown along with her body. As a result, the blood supply to her extremities was extremely poor.

My mother was gone most of the summer of 1962. She was hospitalized in Chapel Hill, which is ninety or so miles from where we lived. Dad would work all day, and right after he came home and showered, usually without even eating, he drove to be with Mother. He wouldn't get home until after midnight.

My parents had made an addition to our house, two bedrooms and a half bath. It was much needed, as I had been sleeping on a cot in the living room so my sister could have her own room. To save money, I did all of the painting of the addition, inside and out. I finished the outside in early summer, while carpenters did the dry walling and the plumbing was installed. During the time my mother was away, I worked on the inside, putting two coats of white paint in the hall, the bedrooms, and the bathroom. I was determined to have those rooms looking nice and pretty when my mother came home from the hospital.

I remember painting those walls day after day, the fresh sheetrock

sucking the thick white liquid from the roller like a sponge ab-
sorbs water. It seemed to take forever to cover a small section of
gray wall and make it look bright and new. Summertime in the
sandhills of North Carolina meant high temperatures with humidity to match. We didn't have air conditioning in our house,
but a small floor fan helped. I had it pointed away from me so
the paint didn't dry before it left my roller.

Baseball was what kept me going. My daytime companion
was a little cream-colored plastic radio. I had won it at school by
selling magazine subscriptions to raise money for playground
equipment. That radio played constantly, and it seemed like
Pat Boone blasted out "Why don't you come home, Speedy
Gonzalez" at least six times every day. In the afternoons, Mutual Radio aired the major league Game of the Day, and that
made my seemingly endless work bearable. Listening to those
games made the days go faster, and sometimes I was surprised
at how much of a wall I had covered by the time the bottom of
the ninth rolled around.

The best times for me were always when I was wearing my
baseball glove or holding a bat. Our Babe Ruth League team
practiced every Saturday and played two nights during the week.
It was usually ninety-five degrees or hotter when we practiced,
but I didn't care. Baseball was always fun.

My coach, an easy-going man named Larry Green, helped me
become a decent hitter instead of just a walk-begging batter. After watching me take pitch after pitch with the bat stuck on my
shoulder the first few games of my first Babe Ruth League season, Larry changed me forever. One night, before our game, he
called me to the side and said, "I'm batting you leadoff. Tonight,
I want you to swing at any pitch you can reach. I don't want you
to get any walks. I don't care if you strike out, I don't care if you
get a base hit. But if you take a single called strike, I am pulling
you out of the game."

That night, I flied to short center, looped a single to left, grounded
out to second, and bounced a single up the middle. I was thrilled.
From that time on, I swung the bat and got my share of hits.

Our team finished second in the standings all three of my seasons in the six-team Babe Ruth League. I played quite a bit in the outfield during that time, spending most of my time at second and first base. I batted .293 my first year, .375 the next, and .452 my final season. Despite my improvement at the plate, I was no finished product as a hitter. The good thing was that I swung the bat, and I usually made contact. I hardly ever struck out. Being a left-handed batter, I worked hard at the drag bunt, and I used it, as well as regular bunts, effectively. The field we played on had a dirt infield, and without grass, it was difficult to deaden the ball. But I could push bunts down the third-base line and drag them past the pitcher between the first and second basemen.

As a leadoff hitter, I continued to draw a lot of walks, reach base frequently, and score quite a few runs. My arm, always accurate, grew stronger. I became a better fielder as I learned to get my shoulders squarely in front of ground balls hit to my right instead of backhanding so many of them. Dad was the reason for that improvement, staying after practice with me several times and hitting hundreds of ground balls to my right, reminding me to move my feet and get in front of the ball. I became a dependable infielder, and I was no longer a liability at the plate.

My mother suffered through a series of amputations. She lost a toe, a couple more toes, part of her left foot, the entire foot, and, eventually, her left leg. That was when I was in high school. While I was in college, her right leg was removed.

Mother spent the last twenty-one of her sixty-three years in a wheelchair. And, while that may have slowed her in terms of locomotion, it did nothing to cool her burning desire to do something with her life. After losing both legs, she began painting and became an accomplished artist, winning ribbons at juried art shows and selling many of her works. At the age of fifty-two, she realized a lifelong dream of attending college, finishing in three years and graduating with highest honors. She then taught grammar school children to read, working miracles with kids who had learning problems, until she died. She had such great spirit, grit, and determination, always moving forward rather than looking back.

When I think of my mother, I always think of Dad, too. He

was such a strong person, physically and emotionally. He was totally committed to Mother and to my sister and me. Everything he did was for us.

Chapter 8
Ted

The Splendid Splinter makes a
lasting impression

I always liked Ted Williams. Despite the spitting. Despite the profanity. Despite the tantrums. In fact, in a way, I liked him because of those things. They were as much a part of him as his poetic swing.

His temper and the fact that he pouted just made him more human. Williams — also known as the Splendid Splinter, the Kid, Teddy Ballgame, and the Thumper — never tried to be what he wasn't, never tried to play a role for the public. His reactions to crowds' boos and taunts and to sports writers' scathing words, which were often unfair and sometimes downright untrue, reflected Williams' honesty.

He did not campaign to be the media's darling, did not play politics. He let people know what he thought and felt. His actions, although immature, were the only way he had of expressing his feelings, his only way of fighting back. I certainly do not condone those actions, but I do understand them.

After all, what was more immature — Williams thumbing his nose and spitting at fickle fans or the mean-spirited newspaper writers holding a grudge over Ted's insults and refusing to give him even a tenth-place Most Valuable Player vote when his statistics warranted being presented the award?

I never saw Williams play; at least, not in person. And I only saw him on television a few times. I remember watching a game with my daddy, and when Williams came to bat, Dad said, "This man may be the best hitter to play in the big leagues. Ever. Just watch him — the way he swings, how he will never go for a bad pitch. And his confidence. You can see it on the TV screen. Ted Williams can hit."

I really admired Williams, and over the years, as I have read everything written about him that I could find, I have felt an even stronger admiration and a certain affection. I have read many, many accounts of his charitable deeds (which he went out of his way to keep private) and his kindness, both to children and other players. I was touched by his Hall of Fame induction speech in which he lobbied for the Cooperstown inclusion of the greats from the Negro League era.

Williams was consistent. He remained true to himself. In 1959, he pinched a nerve in his neck just before spring training began. Pain and stiffness, which prevented him from turning his head to see the ball properly when hitting, persisted the entire season. It was his lone bad season in a nineteen-year career. He batted .254, the only time in those nineteen seasons that his average was lower than .316.

The Boston Red Sox were paying him $125,000 a year. When Williams visited the office of Dick O'Connell, the team's general manager, he was told his contract would be exactly the same. Ted said, that, no, he would not play for that amount of money. He pointed out that he had received the largest raise in baseball and that, now, after having a bad year, he deserved the largest pay cut. He did not mention the stiff, painful neck which plagued him all season. He signed for $90,000, a reduction of $35,000. Imagine a player today doing that. Williams, who turned forty-two in August, went out and hit .316 with 29 home runs in his final season.

The only time the Red Sox played in the World Series during Williams' career was in 1946, when they lost to the St. Louis Cardinals in seven games. Boston clinched the American League pennant early that year, while the Cardinals had to beat the Brooklyn Dodgers in a best-of-three playoff to win the National League flag. While waiting to learn which team they would meet in the Series, the Red Sox played three exhibition games against a team of American Leaguers. In one of them, Williams was hit by a pitch on the point of his elbow. It ballooned up, continued to hurt him, and affected his swing. He batted .200 for the Series, with no extra-base hits and one RBI.

Crushed with disappointment, Williams cried after the seventh game and blamed himself for Boston's defeat. Again, he made no excuses. And, again, he did not feel he deserved money when he did not produce. He signed over his entire World Series share, thousands of dollars, to the Red Sox clubhouse man, Johnny Orlando.

I think those two incidents speak volumes about Ted Williams' character.

I never served in the military. My daddy did. He was overseas for the entirety of World War II. I have always felt that everyone who served during that war, as well as wars before and since, were and are heroes. Williams served a total of five years in two wars. After the 1942 season, he enlisted in naval aviation and served as a flight instructor. He missed three full seasons, when he was twenty-four through twenty-six years old, and one has to believe Ted would have enjoyed very big seasons at those ages. Then, when he was thirty-three, he was called to active duty for the Korean War six games into the 1952 season.

Many major leaguers in the military played for service teams during wars. Williams flew combat missions over Korea. He was hit during one run, and he crash-landed his jet and dove from the flaming plane. He contracted pneumonia a short while after that and was sent back to the United States, having flown thirty-nine missions.

When The Grass Turns Green

Like everybody else who knows even a little bit about baseball, I marvel at what might have been had he not lost five seasons during the prime of his career. Some simple math and extremely conservative estimates indicate Williams would have set several additional records. It brought a lump to my throat when I heard him say that he really did not feel robbed by missing those opportunities, that, instead, he felt privileged to have had the chance to serve his country.

Williams was my model as a hitter as I'm sure he was for probably thousands of youngsters hoping the Splendid Splinter's magic might somehow transform them into terrific hitters. His book, The Science of Hitting, makes so much sense, breaking down the mechanics of batting and explaining the reason behind his thinking. Like everything, though, talent is required to turn solid fundamentals into greatness.

Williams possessed more talent than most when it came to hitting a baseball. He also worked harder at it than perhaps anyone who has come down the pike. He stood in front of a mirror, with or without a bat, and practiced his swing. He might jump up from bed in the middle of the night, and standing in the darkness, work on turning his hips into a pitch or adjusting something in his stance that would make him feel more balanced. It has been said that he was obsessed with hitting. Perhaps. But I think he loved hitting so much and that he was the kind of person who could not accept anything short of perfection. He knew perfection was not possible, but he was driven to strive toward it. He was the same way when it came to tying flies, fishing, and piloting an airplane.

That drive led Williams to arrive at Fenway Park early in the morning on the day of a night game and get whomever he could find to throw him extra batting practice. When he sensed there was something not quite right in his swing, he would hit and hit and hit, sometimes raising blisters on his hands. There were no batting gloves when he played, and I doubt Teddy Ballgame would have worn them anyway. When the blisters bled, he would hit some more. The pain of a slump was, for him, far more dreadful than a few blisters.

Williams' hard work paid off with the recognition he craved; he is generally acknowledged as the greatest hitter who ever lived. He won two triple crowns (.356 average, 36 home runs, 137 RBI in 1942;

.343, 32, 114 in 1947. He batted .344 and slugged 521 homers over his career. His .482 on-base percentage is the best of all time. His slugging percentage of .634 is second only to Babe Ruth.

Williams was his own worst enemy. His determination to be the best drove him to lofty heights; it also left him inwardly hurting, pained when he fell short. There were times when he got three hits in four at-bats, only to walk the streets angrily after the game as he stewed with self-contempt over the out he had made. Never giving pitchers credit for getting him out, he chastised himself for a poor swing or for going after a pitch he thought was a bad one.

I loved a lot about Ted Williams. One of the things was the way he ran around the bases when he hit a home run. He put his head down, appearing a bit self-conscious, and trotted to first, picking up speed as he headed toward second, and completed the circuit as if he was in a hurry to get back to the dugout. And he probably was. Knowing he had hit the ball squarely was the reward for him; he did not need to bask in the crowd's adulation. He never came out for a curtain call, never raised his fist to the skies or held up a finger to signify he was number one. Everyone in baseball already knew that.

Since his death in 2002, people have learned more and more about the compassion of this great American hero. His tireless work for more than fifty years for the Jimmy Fund was well documented. He always wanted to help children who were in bad health or who had unfortunate circumstances. There were many more instances when Williams gave his time and his money. For example, he learned of several former ball players who had not qualified to receive checks from the game's pension fund, and he deposited personal checks for thousands of dollars into their bank accounts.

Ted Williams' hitting spoke for itself. As did his records and the way he went about his life. He was not determined to just be the best hitter. He wanted to be the best pilot and the best fisherman and the best hunter. When he set out to do something, he would read everything he could find about the subject and question people with experience and expertise in that area. He wanted to learn everything he possibly could.

In fact, he was that way about history and politics, too. Williams' biggest regret was not having more education. He talked often about the value of knowledge and attaining it. He wished he had gone to college. Because he had not, he spent a considerable amount of time educating himself. Not to impress anybody, but because he was hungry to learn. And he likely knew a whole lot more about a whole lot of things than some folks with degrees hanging on their walls.

Those who follow baseball know about Williams' .406 batting average in 1941. They know about his refusal to sit out a doubleheader the final day of that season to preserve the cherished .400 figure. They know that he went out and got six hits in eight at-bats. Those episodes are like huge granite monuments in baseball folklore. I have read the events of the final day of Williams' 1941 season over and over again. Batting .400 is one of the most illustrious feats in all of sports history. No one has done it since Teddy Ballgame did it.

Yet, I do not rate it as Ted Williams' greatest accomplishment.

For me, that was his .388 season in 1957. The Splendid Splinter was thirty-nine years old when the season ended. And he missed another mystical .400 by just five hits.

FIVE HITS! At a time when he couldn't run a lick, when infielders played him deep into the outfield grass and took away base hits. If he could have run even a little bit, he likely would have legged out five more hits.

Williams had 38 home runs, a .526 on-base percentage, and a .731 slugging percentage to go with his .388 batting average in 1957. What a season for anyone, but what a miraculous season for an old man ... in baseball years and for a position player.

Still, when one thinks about all of the dramatics he staged, it was just more typical Ted.

Chapter 9
Silencing Sixties' Bats

New rules mark a new day for pitchers

In a decade marked by astounding hitting feats, pitching was the most definitive element of baseball in the 1960s. The pitching was not just very good; it was dominating. Earned run averages were low, and so were batting averages. Thirty-four no-hitters were thrown during the decade, and pitchers set records that still have not been broken. Twenty men who pitched in the 1960s wound up in the Hall of Fame. And, while talent might seem explanation enough for such tremendous accomplishments, there was more to it than that.

On January 26, 1963, members of major league baseball's rules committee met with an agenda to give pitchers a boost, and they voted to expand the strike zone. Until then, a pitch had been defined as a strike if it crossed the plate between a batter's armpits and the top of his knees. The new strike zone included the area from a batter's shoulders to the bottom of his knees. Committee members noted that they were only returning the strike zone to the way it had been before 1950. However, a history check revealed that the strike zone at that time was from a batter's knees to his shoulders. The key wording of the new rule was "from the bottom of the knees" as opposed to "the knees."

Roger Maris, a shy guy who never liked being noticed, was a factor in the rules being changed. Major League Baseball Commissioner Ford Frick did not want the New York Yankees' right fielder to break Babe Ruth's single-season record of 60 home runs set in 1927. Maris and teammate Mickey Mantle were both on a torrid home run pace in 1961, and Maris ended up hitting 61, Mantle 54. Frick, who had once been a ghost writer for Ruth, said in July of that season that any player hitting more than 60 home runs in 154 games would be cited as holding the new record. (Teams had played 154 games in a season until 1961 expansion increased schedules to 162 games.)

The Commissioner added that if a player hit the 60 mark after his team had played 154 games, there would have to be some distinctive mark in the record books. Following Frick's announcement, New York sportswriter Dick Young suggested an asterisk be used as the "distinctive mark," but that did not actually happen. Record books simply used footnotes to denote the extra games. There was never an infamous asterisk placed by Maris's name. It is only mythical.

His 61 home runs played a role in rules being changed. But that was just an underlying part of the motivation behind widening the strike zone and helping the pitchers. There was a feeling around baseball — again, originating with Frick — that offenses were too potent. It was feared that offense was taking over the game, that too many runs were being scored, and that home runs had become cheap.

In 1962, 3,001 homers were hit in the major leagues, a record at that time. Frick, who even said he would like to see the spitball brought back, thought the balance between pitchers and hitters was out of whack and that pitchers were in desperate need of help. Influenced by the Commissioner, the rules committee returned to what was called "the old strike zone." Adding an inch or two at the bottom of the strike zone would hopefully induce more ground balls, while producing fewer fly balls, therefore fewer homers.

From a hitter's standpoint, the new strike zone definitely made it tougher, particularly on lower pitches. "I could tell a tremendous difference," said George Altman, who batted over .300 in back-to-back seasons in the early 1960s while playing for the Chicago Cubs. "I am 6-foot-4, and they were calling pitches down at my ankles — very low strikes. The strike zone got bigger, and then it got exaggerated. That made it rough on us hitters, especially against guys like Gibson, Koufax, and Drysdale. They were tough enough as it was."

The desired result was attained immediately. Total runs scored and bases on balls issued in the majors both decreased by twelve percent in 1963, and home runs dropped by nearly ten percent. The batting average for the National League dipped sixteen points and it was eight points lower in the American League. Meanwhile, strikeouts increased by eight percent, pushing the ratio of the number strikeouts to every walk from 1.6 in 1962 to 2.0 the next year. The majors' collective earned run average fell by exactly half of a run. Runs, home runs, batting averages, and ERAs continued their downward spiral. Batting averages for the National and American Leagues as a whole sank below .250 ten times (of a possible twelve) from 1963-68.

The period from 1963 until the early 1970s was known in baseball as the Second Dead-Ball Era. The first, which lasted from 1901-1919, was characterized by offenses built around speed. There were few power hitters in the major leagues during that time, and home runs were almost non-existent. Thirteen times during the two decades, a league leader in home runs hit fewer than ten of them. The 1908 Chicago White Sox, who finished twenty-four games above .500, had a .224 team batting average and a meager total of three home runs. Huge ballparks encouraged offenses to bunt, hit and run, and steal bases, utilizing speed as their primary weapon. The same baseball was sometimes used for nearly 100 pitches in a game, and the spitball was legal, two more factors in the low scoring.

Pitchers' enormous overall success during the 1960s defied logic in one respect as four new teams were added early in the decade. Four more were added in the second shot of expansion, which took place in 1969. So, four expansion teams played most of the 1960s, meaning that anywhere from forty to fifty pitchers were needed to stock those franchises. Logically, expansion dilutes pitching because the additional pitchers would not be in the majors without it. Of course, a few of the pitchers in question might prove to be very good, having only needed the opportunity to prove it.

Normally, though, more is less when it comes to the number of pitchers throwing in the major leagues. It stands to reason, then, that hitters would benefit from feeding off of expansion teams — at least, in the first few years of their existence. As a result, offensive numbers would be bloated during that period as would earned run averages.

That, however, did not happen. The American League first expanded in 1961, adding the Washington Senators and Los Angeles Angels. In 1960, the eight American League teams batted a collective .255, while pitchers had a 3.87 ERA. In 1961, American League hitters had a .256 batting average, and it fell to .247 in 1963. The American League earned run average was 4.02 in 1961 and .3.63 in 1963. National League expansion began in 1962, adding the New York Mets and Houston Colt .45s. In 1961, the eight National League teams batted a collective .262. In 1962, National League hitters combined for a .261 batting average, followed by .245 in 1963. The league earned run average in 1961 was 4.52, dropping to 4.48 in the first year of expansion and to 3.81 in 1963.

These statistics should not be misinterpreted to indicate that the additional pitchers forced into action by expansion necessarily improved the overall quality of pitching. The conclusion, instead, is that the new strike zone was the reason for the drop in those numbers. Notice that batting averages and ERAs were down in both leagues the first year of the larger strike zone.

Back in 1950, the major league rules committee shrunk the strike zone — from the batter's armpits to the top of the knees — and offenses flourished. The best league earned run average for a season during that decade was 3.67, and league earned run averages ballooned near or above 4.00 thirteen times. The big league batting average for the ten-year period was right at .260, and the 1950 Boston Red Sox hit .302 as a team.

Another huge advantage for pitchers during most of the 1960s was a high mound. A 1950 rule set pitcher's mounds at a standard fifteen inches, but there was no enforcement, and the mounds in some ballparks were extremely high. Six-foot-five Don Drysdale and six-two Sandy Koufax of the Dodgers comprised one of the most intimidating and most successful pitching combos in baseball history. As formidable as they were, there were reports that they got some extra "home cooking" in Los Angeles, where the mound was built up particularly high. A glance at the pair's earned run averages tends to support the theory that something was up. Koufax and Drysdale combined for earned run averages of 1.98, 2.01, 1.46, 1.89, and 2.01 in Dodger Stadium from 1962-66. Their combined ERAs on the road were more than a run higher in each of those five years, with the exception of 1963.

Altman, the only left-handed batter to hit two home runs in one game off of Koufax, felt the new rules had an effect on him. Stats support Altman. After batting .318 and .303, totaling 48 home runs and 170 RBI in 1961 and 1962, he fell to .274 and .230 in 1963 and 1964, with nine homers and 47 runs batted in each year.

"Some of those mounds looked like mountains," Altman said, laughing. "The one in Los Angeles seemed pretty high to me. Koufax would stand up there and throw that big over-hand curveball, and it just went straight down, like it was rolling off the table. Again, he had overpowering stuff and didn't need any help, but the higher mound made him practically unhittable."

The ballparks were also an important factor. During the 1960s, almost every park was pitcher friendly. The only real exception was Atlanta Fulton County Stadium. Dodger Stadium in Los Angeles, the Astrodome in Houston, Cleveland's Municipal Stadium, New York's Shea Stadium, McAfee Coliseum in Oakland, Busch Stadium in St. Louis, and Candlestick Park in San Francisco all had expansive foul territory that provided a lot of extra outs. Home runs were harder to come by as fences were farther from home plate and the carry of the ball was not particularly good anywhere other than Atlanta and, for some day games, Shea Stadium. Chicago's Wrigley Field has been a home run haven when the wind is blowing out, but it frequently blows into home plate, making it difficult to get a ball out of the park.

The increase in night games also helped pitchers. Batters did not see the ball as well under the lights, and the ball carried better in the daytime. Fielders began using larger gloves, which meant more balls could be caught, thus improving defenses. More advantages for pitchers.

Chapter 10
Pitching Prevails

Dominating performances highlight decade

For several years in the 1960s, an inordinate number of pitchers strung together ridiculously successful seasons. It all came to a head in one sensational summer.

In 1968 — The Year of the Pitcher — the collective major league earned run average plummeted to 2.98, and almost twenty-one percent of all games were shutouts. Twenty teams combined to hit 1,995 home runs, just 891 of those coming in the National League. The National League batting average was .243, the American League's was .230. Twenty-one pitchers posted ERAs of 2.50 and lower.

Carl Yastrzemski's .301 in 1968 was the lowest average ever to win a batting title, and he was one of only six players in the majors to hit .300. Roberto Clemente placed tenth in the National League batting race, his .291 marking the only time in his final thirteen big league seasons that the Pittsburgh right fielder failed to hit at least .312.

Pitchers' supremacy reached a pinnacle in 1968. There were several premier performances that season, but Bob Gibson was in a world of his own. The Cardinals' right-hander won 22 games, pitched 13 shutouts, completed 28 starts, and had a 1.12 earned run average, the lowest in the major leagues in fifty-four years. (Left-hander Dutch Leonard of the Boston Red Sox had a 0.96 in 1914.) No one has approached that ERA since. Gibson's innings pitched total exceeded his hits allowed by more than 100. He was a unanimous choice for the National League Cy Young Award and was also the Most Valuable Player.

Gibson was a superb athlete, one who was very serious and fiercely competitive. After a childhood plagued by health issues that included asthma, pneumonia, rickets, and a heart murmur, he rose to sports prominence. At Omaha (Nebraska) Technical High School, he was a standout in track, basketball, and as a catcher for the baseball team. Gibson received a basketball scholarship to Creighton University, where he also played shortstop and the outfield in baseball.

The St. Louis Cardinals signed Gibson in 1957, and in the off-season, he played basketball for a while with the barnstorming Harlem Globetrotters. Cards general manager Bing Devine wanted his young pitcher to quit basketball, so he raised Gibson's pay the same amount that the Globetrotters were paying him. Gibson became a regular member of the St. Louis starting rotation when Johnny Keane took over as manager midway through the 1961 season.

"Bob Gibson threw everything hard," former big league outfielder George Altman said. "He didn't throw that many off-speed pitches. You knew it was going to be a sinking fastball or a slider with him, but it didn't matter because he put the ball where he wanted it. He threw a heavy ball, too, so when you hit it, you didn't often hit it well. Sometimes it felt like he was knocking the bat out of your hands. And he didn't mind pitching inside."

As overpowering as his 1968 performance was, there was nothing more impressive than Gibson's showings in three World Series during the decade. October provided him a stage, and he was the star.

He pitched two complete-game wins in the 1964 Series, striking out 31 batters in 27 innings as St. Louis defeated the Yankees. Gibson missed eight weeks of the 1967 season after his leg was broken by a line drive off the bat of Clemente. The right-hander came back in September, won his last two decisions, and started the World Series opener against the Red Sox. He took the loss, but bounced back to win twice, including the decisive seventh game. He was the Series MVP, just as he had been in 1964. In nine career World Series starts, Gibson was 7-2, with eight complete games and 92 strikeouts in 81 innings.

Also in 1968, Denny McLain, Detroit's combustible right-hander, became the first major league pitcher to win thirty games since Dizzy Dean did it for the St. Louis Cardinals' Gashouse Gang in 1934. McLain's 31-6 record included 28 complete games and a 1.96 ERA. The most victories for a pitcher since then has been 27 by the Phillies' Steve Carlton in 1972 and by Oakland's Bob Welch in 1990.

Gibson and McLain hooked up twice in the 1968 World Series. Gibson pitched a pair of five-hitters, setting a Series record with 17 strikeouts in the opener, then whiffing ten Tigers and hitting a home run in Game Four. McLain did not last past the fifth inning in absorbing two losses, but he came back on two days' rest to go the distance in Detroit's Game Six pounding of the Cardinals. That evened things at three wins apiece and set the stage for a fitting climax to the Year of the Pitcher.

Mickey Lolich was an unlikely hero. Listed at 200 pounds and looking heavier, the southpaw pitched in the shadows of the astonishing McLain throughout the 1968 season. Lolich had the reputation of being somewhat of a flake, a laid-back sort who loved motorcycles. Lolich frequently rode one of his bikes twenty miles to Tiger Stadium for day games, hoisting his feet onto the handlebars to avoid getting his pants wet when he zipped through mud puddles. He lost his spot in the rotation for much of August, picked up four wins in relief in ten days, and won six of his last eight starts to post a 17-9 record.

Lolich threw complete-game victories in Games Two and Five of the World Series, and, since he had only had two days' rest, he never expected to get the ball in Game Seven. Mayo Smith asked Lolich if he could pitch five innings, and when he did, the Detroit manager kept begging for one more and one more. Lolich outdueled Gibson, going the distance and hurling an eight-hitter to steal the show and the Series MVP award. No pitcher has won three games in a World Series since.

One of the crowning achievements of 1968 came from another pitcher who did not mind throwing inside. Don Drysdale was an intimidating right-hander, especially tough on right-handed batters with his sidearm delivery that appeared to be coming from third base. On May 14, the 6-foot-5 "Big D" warmed up to pitch against the Chicago Cubs, having been victimized by anemic run support from his Dodger teammates. His record was 1-3, with Los Angeles having scored a total of nine runs in his last eight starts. Drysdale threw a two-hitter at the Cubs that day and won, 1-0, to start a streak that would make history.

Drysdale then pitched another 1-0 gem, beating Houston. Next up were the Cardinals and Gibson, who allowed one hit over eight innings, but the Dodgers scratched out a 2-0 win. Facing the Astros again, Drysdale got plenty of runs for a change. He had to escape two ninth-inning jams — two on and nobody out, and bases loaded and two outs — before winning, 5-0, to stretch his scoreless inning string to thirty-six.

In his next start, Drysdale was leading the Giants, 3-0, after eight innings in front of a large crowd at Dodger Stadium, when it appeared that the streak was in serious jeopardy. Two walks and a single loaded the bases with nobody out, and when Drysdale plunked San Francisco catcher Dick Dietz on the arm with a fastball, it looked like the streak was over.

However, plate umpire Harry Wendelstedt ruled that Dietz had made no attempt to avoid being hit, and he called the pitch a ball, making the count 3-2. The Giants were livid, and an argument of nearly ten minutes ensued. When play resumed, Dietz flied to short right field, Ty Cline grounded into a force out at the plate, and Jack Hyatt popped out. That made five straight shutouts and forty-five consecutive scoreless innings for Drysdale.

He pitched a record sixth shutout in a row and broke Carl Hubbell's National League record of forty-six and a third scoreless innings when he three-hit the visiting Pirates, 5-0. On June 8, with more than 50,000 in attendance at Dodger Stadium, Drysdale put up four more zeroes before the Phillies scored with two outs in the fifth. His fifty-eight and two-thirds consecutive scoreless innings broke Walter Johnson's major league record of fifty-six. (Another Dodger, Orel Hershiser, set the new record of fifty-nine successive scoreless innings in 1988.) Drysdale continued to get few runs with which to work, finishing the season at 14-12 despite a 2.15 ERA.

A year later, Drysdale's career was over. A 5-4 record and shoulder trouble prompted him to retire from baseball in August of 1969 at the age of thirty-three.

The height of mounds was not measured with any regularity until 1969. That was the first season after the rules committee made another set of changes involving pitchers. The committee met in San Francisco following the 1968 season, with the goal to restore some offense to baseball. Owners wanted to put more fans in the seats, and it was their opinion that fans liked seeing runs scored and especially liked watching home runs being hit. The general feeling was that fans looked at pitchers' duels and low-scoring games as boring, and that if the trend of pitching predominance continued, attendance would suffer.

So, mounds were lowered from fifteen to ten inches. Five inches, or one-third of the previous height, was an enormous reduction. The strike zone was also reduced, returning to the 1950 edict of armpits to the top of the knees. There would also be more strict enforcement of rules prohibiting pitchers from using foreign substances on the ball. And, if a pitcher put his hand to his mouth while standing on the mound, a ball would be called.

Pitching has changed drastically in the past twenty-five years, and specialization is a major reason. Whereas starting pitchers frequently either worked deep into games or finished them through the 1970s, twenty-first century pitchers seldom last nine innings. The "quality start" — a term that has evolved into an actual statistic — has replaced the complete game as the goal of most starting pitchers. Concocted by sportswriter John Lowe in 1985, a quality start is awarded to a starter who pitches at least six innings and allows three or fewer earned runs.

Tough old birds like Spahn, Early Wynn, and Robin Roberts would have been insulted by such a meager expectation, probably arguing that the only quality start was a complete-game victory. Their determination to finish what they started made managers sometimes think twice before walking to the mound to make a pitching change. Those pitchers, and many more like them, took considerable exception to visits from managers, and starters sometimes became more than a little angry when they were removed from games. They pitched more innings, completed more games, and earned more victories.

An extension of pitchers' mindsets years ago was that, in focusing on nine innings as the prize, there was no talk of pitch counts. Starters' limits were normally whatever number of pitches was required to get twenty-seven outs. Obviously, there were days when starters were knocked out of the box, but there were also days when they would go the distance and take a loss.

Part of the reason for that was the pitchers' feeling there was no one better than them to get the job done. Part of it, too, was that relief pitchers were often viewed somewhat as "second-class citizens," the idea being that if they were not good enough to start, they were not dependable enough to be called on in tense situations. Starting pitchers did not like being replaced by guys like that. It was literally embarrassing for some pitchers when they were taken out of games.

One of the factors in what is construed of as the "babying" of today's pitchers is the amount of money teams have invested in them, and the desire to protect that investment. When a team shells out millions of dollars for a youngster before he ever throws a pitch, management understandably wants to take every possible precaution to prevent injuries.

Also, there has been the belief that, with the increase to thirty major league teams, the overall pitching in the big leagues has been weakened. Scouts and managers have felt youngsters are often rushed to the majors before they are ready. The bottom line is that there have been a large number of minor league (in terms of experience and preparation) pitchers on major league pitching staffs.

Set-up men and one-inning closers have glorified — and enriched

— members of the bullpen, while diminishing starting pitchers' expectations. "Get me to the sixth or seventh" is a popular manager's cry nowadays. It used to be, "Here are the ball and the game. Get us a W." When they get into a jam, starters are quick to look to the dugout. They are not conditioned to work out of trouble on a regular basis, so they do not think that way.

The modern-day closer almost always comes into games in the ninth inning with no one on base and often with a two- or three-run lead. The situations are much more comfortable than most of the ones in which Hoyt Wilhelm and Elroy Face normally found themselves. Both frequently pitched two innings or longer to notch a save.

The same was true of Rollie Fingers, who made a name for himself in the 1970s before winning the 1981 American League MVP and Cy Young awards with 41 saves and a 1.04 ERA. After pitching one and a third innings in his only 1968 major league game, he averaged fifty-nine appearances over his remaining sixteen seasons.

Wilhelm was the first relief pitcher inducted into the Hall of Fame (1985). He was followed by Fingers, Dennis Eckersley (who was a starter for the first half of his career), Bruce Sutter, and Goose Gossage. Lee Smith is a mystery Hall of Fame omission in light of his 478 saves.

There were less than 14,000 fans in Candlestick Park on July 19, 1960, when San Francisco right-hander Juan Marichal made his major league debut against the visiting Philadelphia Phillies. It took only two hours and seven minutes to play the game, which Marichal dominated. He struck out a dozen Phillies, walked one, and allowed one hit, a two-out single by pinch-hitter Clay Dalrymple in the eighth inning. The Giants won, 2-0.

Marichal would go on to throw 51 more shutouts, become a six-time 20-game winner, and post a 2.69 earned run average in a career which would earn him the nickname Dominican Dandy and a plaque in Cooperstown.

"He had four or five pitches, all with different speeds," said George Altman, "and he kept hitters off balance; he could tie you up in knots. Definitely a guy I had rather not face."

Characterized by his high leg kick and pinpoint control, Marichal led the National League in 1968 with 26 wins, and his 191 victories were the most by any major league pitcher in the 1960s. Yet, he did not receive a single vote on annual ballots for the Cy Young Award during the decade.

Luis Tiant always had pizzazz. Sporting a Fu Manchu mustache that became one of his trademarks along with a head-bobbing wind-up during which he completely turned his back to batters, he celebrated victories with a large grin and a larger cigar. Known as El Tiante, he was another outstanding pitcher who was a product of the 1960s. The right-hander, whose father had been a star pitcher in the Negro Leagues, became a headliner in his fifth season with the Cleveland Indians after they purchased his contract from the Mexican League.

Tiant was one more pitcher who had a remarkable 1968. He led the American League with a 1.60 earned run average, pitched nine shutouts, struck out 264 in 258 and one-third innings, and went 21-9. That was the first of his four 20-win seasons. His 229 career victories are the most for a Cuban-born pitcher.

Tiant, who is not in the Hall of Fame, won 20 more big league games than Drysdale, whose plaque is in Cooperstown. Both pitched 49 shutouts and more than 3,400 innings. Tiant was 2-0 with a shutout in his only World Series, his Red Sox losing to Cincinnati in 1975. Drysdale was 3-3 with a shutout in five World Series, three of which the Dodgers won.

Certainly a Cooperstown case could be made for Tiant as well as a couple of left-handers whose careers spanned the entirety of the 1960s. Tommy John had a lifetime 288-231 record, a 3.34 earned run average, and a 6-2 postseason record that included a 2-1 mark in five World Series starts. Jim Kaat's lifetime record was 283-237, with a 3.45 ERA, and a 1-2 mark in three World Series starts. Right-hander Bert Blyleven, who arrived in the majors in 1970, must be mentioned in the same breath: 287-250, 3.31, 3,701 strikeouts, 60 shutouts, and 2-1 in three World Series starts.

Compare those numbers with Hall of Fame member Ferguson Jenkins: 284-226, 3.34 ERA, 49 shutouts, with no post-season appearances.

If the win column is the final destination, John, Kaat, and Blyleven should — considering Jenkins' total — have what it takes to be inducted, even though their winning percentages are slightly lower. Did it take them too long to get there? John spent twenty-six years in the majors, Kaat twenty-five, and Blyleven twenty-two, while Jenkins' career lasted nineteen years. Strikeouts, or the lack of them, could be a factor with John and Kaat as neither reached the 2,500 level, while Jenkins surpassed 3,000. But Blyleven had more strikeouts than Jenkins.

Hall of Fame voting is always ripe for criticism because it is based on opinion. Although there are magic numbers like 3,000 hits and 500 home runs for hitters, and 300 wins and 3,000 strikeouts for pitchers — all of which practically guarantee induction — there really are no set qualifications for entering. Still, when players who are not in the Hall have numbers so similar to players who are, it makes one wonder.

Strangely for John, he is perhaps best known for the surgery named for him as he was the first pro athlete to have the procedure which replaces an elbow ligament with a tendon from another part of the body.

Warren Spahn just did not know when to quit. At least, that is what many writers and fans surmise when using the standard formula on when to retire from a sport. The idea, most people would agree, is for an athlete to leave before his skills do — before he embarrasses himself and replaces memories of greatness with visions of mediocrity or worse. Based on that, Spahn hung around baseball too long.

He had a 6-13 record in 1964, pitching less than 245 innings for the first time in eighteen years and managing just four complete games after averaging 21 over a period of seventeen seasons. But even with those numbers, and perhaps a more telling forty-four (birthdays), Spahn pitched on. Milwaukee sold him to the New York Mets following the season, and the Mets released the old left-hander in July. San Francisco signed him, and although Spahn pitched creditably, the Giants released him after the season.

Even then, he did not retire. Spahn pitched in the Mexican League in 1966 and in the Pacific Coast League in 1967. Criticized for sticking around too long, he said, "I don't care what the public thinks. I'm pitching because I enjoy pitching." When there was nowhere else he could continue doing that, he retired at the age of forty-six. And it was not his idea. "I didn't quit," Spahn said. "Baseball retired me." There is something admirable about a man playing baseball because he loves it, with no fear or concern of tarnishing his image.

It was hard for Spahn to accept that he was finished. And looking at his 1963 season, it is easy to understand why he felt that way. Forty-two at the time, he threw 22 complete games, had a 23-7 record, pitched seven shutouts, and posted a 2.60 earned run average. No wonder he thought he could keep going.

Sandy Koufax knew that he (himself) could not, but his retirement had nothing to do with diminishing skills. In fact, Koufax was in his prime when he called it quits at the age of thirty. His final season was 1966, when he went 27-9, with 27 complete games, five shutouts, 317 strikeouts in 323 innings, and a 1.73 ERA. Those stats earned Koufax his third Cy Young Award — all by unanimous votes — in four years. (Until 1967, there was only one Cy Young Award in all of major league baseball, not one in each league as has been the case since then.)

The only pitcher to retire the year after winning the Cy Young Award, Koufax announced in November of 1966 that his severely arthritic left elbow was forcing him to stop playing. He had endured terrible pain for three seasons, and one doctor said his arm resembled that of a ninety-year-old man. Over the last ten seasons of his twelve-year career, batters hit just .203 against Koufax. He won 97 games, never had an ERA above 2.04, and struck out 1,228 in 1,192.2 innings in his final four seasons. No wonder he became the youngest player (at thirty-six years and twenty-one days) ever elected to the Baseball Hall of Fame.

"To me," Altman said, "Koufax was the number one guy; no doubt about it. He threw that fastball coming at the knees, and when it got to home plate, it was rising. With the kind of speed he had, and then to get so much movement … man, he was something. The next thing you knew, he would throw that curveball that broke straight down.

"Even if you knew what was coming, it didn't help with Koufax. One time, we were playing the Dodgers in Wrigley Field, and he was pitching. We had a player up in the scoreboard getting the signals from the catcher, and he was relaying them to us. That didn't deter Koufax. He struck out twelve or thirteen and shut us out. You would know it was going to be a curve, and you'd make up your mind to swing, and it would break down into the dirt. But we had already started to swing and couldn't stop."

While Spahn has the most wins (363) of any left-hander and Koufax was arguably the greatest, Whitey Ford was the most successful southpaw. Casey Stengel's "money pitcher" for many years, Ford compiled a .69006 winning percentage (236 wins and 106 losses), which is third on the all-time list behind right-handers Spud Chandler (.717) and Dave Foutz (.69014).

His best season was 1961, when he went 25-4 and earned the Cy Young Award. Two years later, he was 24-7. Ford's World Series excellence is one of the reasons he is in the Hall of Fame. He had ten wins and a 2.71 ERA in eleven Series and set a record by pitching thirty-three and one-third consecutive scoreless innings. Ford retired following the 1967 season after winning just two games each of his last two years.

The saddest pitching story of the 1960s — and of any decade, for that matter — was Herb Score and the tragic way his career ended at such a young age. The Cleveland Indians' southpaw flashed Koufax-like stuff before Koufax arrived. Score struck out 508 batters in 477 innings his first two seasons, earning the 1955 American League Rookie of the Year Award. He won 20 his second season.

But on May 7 of 1957, at Cleveland's Municipal Stadium, his promising career was shattered. With two outs in the first inning, a line drive off the bat of the Yankees' Gil McDougald struck Score in the right eye, and he was never the same. He did not pitch again that year and won seventeen games over parts of five frustrating seasons. Score retired four games into the 1962 season, a month before his twenty-ninth birthday.

Of the 34 no-hitters pitched during the 1960s, some stand out. Koufax had a no-no four straight seasons from 1962-65, the last of those a perfect game against the Chicago Cubs. Jim Bunning and Jim "Catfish" Hunter also pitched perfect games during the decade. Spahn threw two no-hitters, and both came after he turned thirty-nine. Both San Francisco and Cincinnati were the sites of back-to-back no-hitters.

On September 17, 1968, Bob Gibson of St. Louis no-hit the Giants, 1-0, in Candlestick Park. The next day, the Cardinals' Ray Washburn again held the Giants hitless, 2-0. In 1969, the Reds and Astros traded no-hitters at Crosley Field. On April 30, Cincinnati's Jim Maloney did not allow a hit in a 10-0 win. On May 1, Houston's Don Wilson pitched a no-hitter in beating the Reds, 4-0.

Pitchers chalked up seventy-two 20-win seasons in the decade, forty-two of them in the National League. Forty-seven pitchers won 20 or more games in a season at least once. Marichal did it six times, Gibson four, with McLain, Koufax, Spahn, Jenkins, and the Yankees' Mel Stottlemyre getting three apiece.

Four of the twenty eventual Hall of Fame pitchers — Wilhelm, Bunning, Gibson, and Marichal — were active throughout the 1960s. Six — Wynn, Spahn, Koufax, Roberts, Drysdale, and Ford — were done by 1967. Gaylord Perry recorded 95 wins during the decade and Jenkins had 75, closing the 1960s with three straight 20-win seasons. Seaver was outstanding in each of his three seasons in the decade. The other seven — Nolan Ryan, Hunter, Fingers, Steve Carlton, Jim Palmer, Phil Niekro, and Don Sutton — made most of their noise in the 1970s.

Chapter 11
Pitchers Talk Pitching

Mr. Met shares mound philosophies

Rules Changes were obviously a factor in the overwhelming success major league pitchers enjoyed during the 1960s. It should not be implied, however, that a more liberal strike zone made pitching a cakewalk. While pitching was outstanding during the decade, it must be remembered that there were some tremendous hitters who were in their prime.

Tom Seaver's rookie season with the New York Mets was 1967, when he won 16 games as a twenty-two-year-old. He recalled how it felt the first time he faced players who had been the objects of his own hero worship.

"Going up against Clemente, Mays, McCovey, and those guys, I don't think I was intimidated," Seaver said. "It's a matter of semantics, but in some cases it was more like awe that I felt. Your childhood dreams and your adult dreams become a reality, and you're thinking this kind of thing really can't be happening to me. Actually, that feeling did not last very long for me.

"I pitched against Aaron in Atlanta for the first time, and I knew his every move — how he held the bat against his belt and put his helmet on when he was getting ready to hit — and I couldn't watch him. I was disciplined enough to know what my job was, so I just turned away until he got into the box. I was trying to control my emotions and not let them overtake me, not let that part of my brain dominate what was going on. The first time I faced him, I ran my sinker in right below the belt buckle, and he hit a grounder to shortstop. Here, I just got Henry Aaron out, and it was hard to keep from showing emotion, but you can't do that.

"Then, we're going around the lineup again, and Henry came up for the second time. And I threw that same kind of pitch, right in there, and I got it right where I wanted it. Only, he didn't stride the same way; he opened up, looked for that pitch, and he hit a home run down the left field line. Adjustment. If there was one lesson that I learned that was most important, it was right there. I said, "Oh, that's why these guys are so good. They can think and adjust. They have the physical ability to be able to do that. That's why these guys excel and excel at a high level for a long period of time."

"You know, in a sense, it was, 'Thank you, Henry Aaron.' The lesson in those two at-bats ratcheted me up ten notches," Seaver said. "The lesson learned was worth the home run. That was forty-something years ago, and I can still see it. That was so important in the education process. The players who continue to do well learn from those experiences. It doesn't take three times or five times. In one little at-bat, there can be a lesson."

Seaver was not the only pitcher to learn from Aaron. Tony Cloninger pitched three and a half years in the Braves' minor league system before being brought up to Milwaukee in the middle of the 1961 season. The twenty-year-old rookie could not have been more excited when he found his locker stuck right between Aaron and Eddie Mathews, both of whom would be elected to the Hall of Fame.

"We had some great veteran pitchers," Cloninger said. "Spahn, Burdette, Buhl … and those guys were really nice to me. They were happy and eager to answer my questions. They wanted to see me succeed. I learned from those guys, but I also learned a whole lot just sitting and listening to Aaron and Mathews. I probably learned as much from them as I did from anyone about how to pitch and what hitters look for in different situations. Teams didn't have all the computerized charts in the dugout like they do now. Those guys watched pitchers, stored information in their heads, and they didn't forget it."

While rules changes provided an advantage for pitchers, they did not totally explain the overwhelming performances of Bob Gibson, Sandy Koufax, Denny McLain, and Juan Marichal.

"The rules weren't the reason," Cloninger said. "Bob Gibson was just so good that I don't care if it would have been today or when, he would have been great. In 1968, he just did whatever he wanted to do. Nobody could touch him. He was one tremendous pitcher. He knew what he was doing out there, he kept hitters off the plate, and then he kept the ball at the knees and on the corners."

Some of the pitchers, after benefiting from a bigger strike zone, were quick to point to the height of the mound being lowered and the shrinking of the strike zone when their earned run averages inflated. But not every pitcher.

"The lower mound was just a physical adjustment," Seaver said, "and I really don't remember anything about the strike zone being different … or, at least, changing anything for me. You always have to be able to adjust, and that was true with mounds because not all of them were the same. They were made of different compositions, so your landing area of your front foot was problematic. Los Angeles had a very heavy clay mound. Atlanta was very soft, so your foot would slide if your timing was incorrect.

"I can't remember any enforcement of the mound height, though. I never saw or heard of anyone measuring mounds. The height of the mound depended on the pitching staff. Grounds crews always manicured the mound to suit the home team's pitchers. Now, there were reports that the mound in L.A. was a little higher, and I wouldn't doubt that one iota."

Cloninger does not have fond memories of the 1968 rule changes. "When they lowered the mounds, that was the thing that hurt the most. It made a difference on your curveball. They narrowed the strike zone, the ballparks started getting smaller, and later, the ball got livelier. It was a great time to be a hitter."

Seaver has his own theories on the difference in pitchers from his era and the ones today. "I think it's more financial than anything else," he said. "Teams put so much money into these guys and don't want them to get hurt, so everyone is very protective. Then, they get hurt anyway. What they do today is look for a reason to take pitchers out.

"Everybody talks about pitch counts. What you do is arbitrarily pick a number. For this guy, just hypothetically, you don't want him throwing over 100 pitches. All of the starters know what their number is. People say, `Oh, this pitch count thing." But I had a pitch count when I pitched; no question about it. My max was about 135. The thing is, I knew without anybody telling me, about where I was. The last three innings, I would know, ballpark anyway, how many pitches I had.

"So, you say to yourself, `How many have I got?" Seaver said. "You have the number eight hitter coming up, and you don't spend eight pitches to get him out. You throw three pitches, and he hits a ground ball to the shortstop … because at other times, you are going to need some pitches to work with. You get Billy Williams up there with runners on first and third, and you are going to need some pitches to work with. That's where you spend them.

"I would say (Jerry) Koosman's count was probably 145, and Nolan (Ryan) could throw 150, 155 pitches. Nolan could throw forever. But we aren't all the same. In the same vein, all pitchers are not the same on the bottom end, either.

"Back then," Seaver said, "if you looked into the dugout, they turned away. I was expected to get out of the jam. Our other starters were, too. That is a learning curve. You struggle, it's the seventh inning, and there is nobody in the bullpen. (Mets manager) Gil Hodges and (pitching coach) Rube Walker are looking at you, and what are they saying? "You're good enough to get out of this." That's what they are saying.

"You make a couple of bad pitches and get yourself in a bad situation, there are runners here and there, and the pitching coach or the manager comes out to the mound. He says, `You're okay. Take a breath, go back to ground zero, go back to the ABCs, and you will get out of this. You're throwing well.' And he pats you on the back and goes back to the dugout, and he sits down and watches. They made you believe that you could do it. And I knew they believed I could do it."

Seaver defined the ABCs of pitching: "A. the first pitch to every batter who walks up there is going to be a strike. At least, that's what you are shooting for, what you want to do. Then, you can get him out on two pitches. B. the first guy who walks up there in the inning is going to be an out. Same theory, and basically, those are the building blocks of pitching excellence; that is the fundamental foundation. C. the guy hitting eighth goes oh for four. It boils down to Thou Shalt Not Dig Thyself a Hole. Thank you very much."

Bob Friend, like Seaver, worked 200 or more innings for eleven consecutive years. Friend was a workhorse for the Pittsburgh Pirates, with whom he spent all but one of his sixteen seasons. He won 197 games, including 22 in 1958 and 18 twice in the 1960s.

"I'm proud of the way I pitched," Friend said. "I went out there and took the ball — I didn't miss a start in fifteen years — and I usually pitched far into the game. I didn't ask out of a start if I felt a little twinge or something in my arm. I always took my turn. I was fortunate not to have any serious arm problems, but I also pitched through some things. I think everybody who pitches has some soreness now and then; that's part of it.

"I think I was durable, both in terms of not missing starts and also in terms of pitching a lot of innings. I don't mean to put today's pitchers down, but back in the 1950s and 1960s, we didn't come out because we had thrown 100 pitches. I don't even think anybody was keeping count. We had to pitch out of a whole lot of jams because managers didn't go to the bullpen as early or as often."

Cloninger, who had 67 wins by the time he was twenty-five, knows about pitching with pain. "I had just had my best year in 1965 (24-11), and then we moved to Atlanta. I pitched on opening night in 1966, and I went 13 innings. The longest I had gone in spring training was six innings, and that opening game was on a cold April night, and it was kind of misting.

"That was the beginning of the end for me. I was so sore, and I wasn't feeling completely right when I came back at Shea Stadium a few days later. I kept taking my turn every fourth day, and it got to be really painful to pitch. It was like a knife cutting through my shoulder every time I went out. It was just survival after that. I never said anything to anybody. Guys didn't do that a whole lot back then. If you did, you would have been out of there as fast as you came in."

Cloninger acknowledged that, "the game has changed. It starts in the minor leagues where pitchers are allowed to throw a limited number of pitches. Teams invest millions of dollars in these kids, and they are going to do everything possible to take care of them. Some of them come out of college and have to be rehabbed right away because they pitched so much for their schools. The complete game is rare now, but that's because nobody expects it. Starters are geared to go six or seven innings, then turn the game over to the set-up guys, and then you've got your closer.

"I do think baseball in the 1960s was special, but part of that was because it was when I played, and all of those big heroes I had read about were playing then. There were a whole bunch of great pitchers back then, and there are some mighty good arms now. Today's pitchers are just asked to do different things than they were when I played."

Cloninger was probably the rule rather than the exception during the 1960s when it came to not revealing that he was in pain. And, although it sounds as if he did further damage to his arm by continuing to pitch, the same might not be true for every pitcher who experiences discomfort. A trip to the disabled list, as Friend suggests, might not always be necessary.

Cloninger pitched 257 innings that 1966 season, giving him 776 in three years. He pitched just 758 more innings over the last six years of his career, which concluded in 1972. Fifteen years later, he began working in the minor leagues with the New York Yankees, and he was the pitching coach with the big club when it won four World Series championships under Joe Torre.

Chapter 12
Black Stars Emerge

Different faces gain stardom
during the sixties

The 1960s is one of the most intriguing periods in major league baseball history because of what happened on and off the field. Many of the game's marvelous moments have gone unmatched over near-ly forty ensuing years. The decade was also a time of tremendous change for our country, reflecting a society that was experiencing both tumult and an awakening of ideas, while finding the boldness to express them.

The use of drugs became prevalent; college campuses rumbled with discontent; Americans were protesting the Vietnam War, while espousing free love and the right to question the status quo. African Americans demanded their rights as United States citizens, as did women. President John F. Kennedy was assassinated. So was his brother, Robert, when he was a candidate for the presidency. Also murdered was Martin Luther King, the man who led the African Americans' charge toward equality.

Baseball in the 1960s paralleled the decade's events that shook the American civilization. The game's rules were altered, first to tame hitters and then to neutralize pitchers. The number of major league teams increased by fifty percent, bringing about a drastic re-structuring of post-season play. Players gained bargaining strength, allowing them to loosen the club owners' slave-like grip, and at the end of the decade, there was a hint of what would become free agency. Highlighting the incredible ten-year period was an explosion of black stars who brought a new level of excitement to baseball.

Jackie Robinson integrated the game in 1947, and the next year, his teammate, Roy Campanella, became the second black to stand out in the major leagues. The following decade saw a parade of black players who quickly achieved star status: first Don Newcombe, then Willie Mays, Ernie Banks, Henry Aaron, and Frank Robinson. A larger wave of black stars emerged in the 1960s.

As a result, glossy pictures of Mays, Aaron, Banks, and Roberto Clemente were tacked onto kids' bedroom walls, walls that previously had been filled solely with photos of Ted Williams, Joe DiMaggio, Stan Musial, and Mickey Mantle, and other white players. Just two decades earlier, a black man playing in a big league game for the first time made headlines. As one black player after another excelled in the major leagues, people stopped keeping count. Although they were clearly in the minority on big league rosters, black players comprised a very high percentage of the stars in the 1960s.

The rosters for the two 1959 All-Star Games included a total of thirteen black players for the American and National Leagues. In 1969, twenty-three blacks were among fifty-nine players selected for one All-Star Game. The difference in those numbers is indicative of the overall increase in black stars in the majors over that ten-year period.

Aaron, Mays, and Newcombe each won an MVP award, Banks took two, and Campanella won three of them in the 1950s. Frank

Robinson also established himself among baseball's elite players, while Clemente, Maury Wills, Orlando Cepeda, and Willie Mc-Covey began paving their roads to stardom.

Seven of the ten National League Most Valuable Players in the 1960s were black, and they were seven different players: Frank Robinson, Wills, Mays, Clemente, Cepeda, Bob Gibson, and McCovey. Black players captured the top four spots in the MVP voting two of those years and comprised four of the top five two other times. Listing the top five players in each year's National League MVP voting to compile a total of fifty for the entire decade (even though some of the names were repeated), twenty-nine of the names belonged to black players. The impressive thing about that is that more than eighty percent of the major league players during the decade were white.

Almost every pennant-winning effort during the 1960s was fueled by spectacular exploits from black players, many of whom were just beginning to flirt with greatness. As the decade progressed, names like Marichal, Brock, Stargell, Morgan, and Gibson grew to be recognized. By 1969, a large number of baseball's so-called household names — the stars — belonged to black players.

George Altman, a two-time National League All-Star, offered an opinion as to why so many black players were standouts in the 1960s. "To tell you the truth, I believe we were just hungry," he said. "Blacks did not have the opportunity to play major league baseball for a long time. When we did, we wanted to be exceptional. I'm not saying the black players were hungrier than the white ones; it's just that we really wanted to take advantage of the chance we had.

"Mays, Aaron, Banks, Clemente, (Frank) Robinson … you could see at first glance that they were great ball players. The thing with them was that they did it year-in and year-out; that's what makes a superstar. We had so many Hall-of-Fame guys in the 1960s. It was a gold mine. That's why I think that was such a special time. The major leagues had just mined the black players, and they were coming to stardom.

"It is pretty amazing that so many of the stars and superstars were black players," Altman said. "A lot of it, I think, had to do with our backgrounds. Although we did not have the facilities many of the white players had, we had to work hard when we were growing up. I chopped wood — it was something I had to do a lot of — and it made me stronger. It was kind of like training, only we didn't know it. We didn't have all of the weight lifting and trainers back then, but most of the black players were strong."

During the 1960s, black players won seven batting championships, all ten home run crowns, and eight RBI titles in the National League. Clemente won each of his four batting titles in the 1960s and led all big league hitters with a .328 average for the decade. Aaron, Mays, and McCovey led or shared the lead in homers three times apiece. Aaron led the entire major leagues with 1,107 RBI during the 1960s, while driving in the most runs in the National League three times. Aaron slammed 375 home runs in the decade, second in the majors behind Harmon Killebrew's 393. Black pitchers were one-two in big league wins for the ten-year period, Juan Marichal recording 191 and Gibson 164. American League black players won four batting titles, one home run crown, and one RBI title during the decade.

Black stars did not appear on the American League horizon as soon or as frequently as in the National League. Perhaps National League owners and general managers felt pressure to keep up with the Dodgers, seeing that their willingness to sign black players was paying off in the wins column. Most of the black stars, and all but a few of the black superstars, of the 1960s played in the National League.

In 1963 — fourteen years after it first happened in the National League — Elston Howard became the first black to win the American League Most Valuable Player Award. There was a bit of irony in that slice of history as Howard was a member of the New York Yankees, whose reluctance to sign black players for so long may have affected other American League teams. Just as National League clubs were influenced by the successful Dodgers, who aggressively pursued and added blacks, American League teams might have figured they should follow the opposite path taken by the mighty Yankees.

Don Buford felt the fact that a large number of blacks excelled in the big leagues during the 1960s was mainly a matter of just getting a chance. He played ten years in the majors, five with the Chicago White Sox and the last five with Baltimore. The Orioles played in three straight World Series with Buford playing left field and batting leadoff. He was selected to the 1971 American League All-Star team.

"Everyone knows there were many outstanding black players a

long time ago," he said, "but they didn't get to play. As to why so many of us were among the better players in the 1960s, I think you would get a better answer by talking to the major league owners and the scouts. You have to talk about baseball providing opportunities. In the 1960s, there was a whole racial situation going on, and that led to black people getting more opportunities in many areas, not just in baseball."

There were two players who were the keys to major league fans accepting black men wearing major league uniforms. One was the Liberator. The other was the Ambassador.

Jackie Robinson was the Liberator. With the help of Brooklyn general manager Branch Rickey, he broke baseball's color barrier on April 15, 1947, when he ran onto Ebbets Field with the Dodgers as they played the Boston Braves. Robinson was twenty-eight when he won the first Rookie of the Year Award ever given. He was the National League MVP two years later when he won the league's batting crown. He hit .311 over ten seasons and stole home nineteen times.

The Ambassador was Willie Mays. He came along four years after Robinson opened the door for black players and was not even the first black on his team, the New York Giants. He oozed good will. Known as the "Say Hey Kid", Mays brought an unmatched exuberance to baseball. His big smile, enthusiasm, and bubbly personality turned people from all walks of life into instant fans.

There is no questioning the importance of Robinson and the Dodgers taking that first step, but it did not insure that the rest of the teams would follow suit in a knee-jerk reaction. Integrating major league baseball was a very slow process. After Robinson's introduction, it took twelve years for the rest of the big league clubs to add the first black player to their rosters.

A multitude of Negro League stars such as Josh Gibson, Buck Leonard, Buck O'Neill, and James "Cool Papa" Bell never had a chance to play at all in the majors. One of the most popular and eternal "what if" baseball discussions wonders just how illustrious their careers might have been had they been spent in the big leagues. Ted Williams shared such feelings during his 1966 induction to the Baseball Hall of Fame. His speech included the following words: "I have been a very lucky guy to have worn a baseball uniform, and I hope some day the names of Satchel Paige and Josh Gibson in some way can be added as a symbol of the great Negro players who are not here only because they weren't given a chance." Williams, who could be profane, was profound that day at Cooperstown, and he proved to be influential. The Hall of Fame, in large part as a reaction to Williams' speech, has recognized thirty-five Negro Leaguers.

Perhaps it was a matter of someone else going first. Maybe it was the combination of character and ability that Robinson displayed, as well as his impact on the Dodgers. Obviously, it was the knowledge that they were missing out on a whole lot of great athletes who could help their teams win. It was likely a combination of all of these factors that led to major league owners and general managers cashing in on the Negro Leagues. As long as the Negro Leagues were in existence, scouting black baseball players was easy, as easy as taking in a game or two and picking someone to sign.

For black baseball fans in cities that had Negro League teams, the integration of the major leagues came at an expensive price. It signaled the end of the Negro Leagues. Once the pipeline opened to the big leagues, and their scouts were instructed to sign black players, they were swooped up. If they did not go directly to the majors, the blacks reported to minor league teams. There was not enough talent left to sustain the Negro Leagues at the level they had maintained throughout their proud, star-laden history, and as attendance dropped, players' salaries did, too. Basically, the leagues became farm teams for major league clubs. The Negro National League folded in 1948, and the Negro American League, although it lasted ten more years, did not boast the individuals or teams it once had.

The Negro Leagues produced fifty-seven major league players. Heading the list are Hall of Famers Aaron, Banks, Campanella, Doby, Monte Irvin, Mays, Paige, and Jackie Robinson.

Altman hit 101 home runs in nine big league seasons, most of them with the Chicago Cubs. He hit a pinch homer in the first 1961 All-Star Game (there were two All-Star Games from 1959-62), and he joined Banks, Billy Williams, and Ron Santo to give the Cubs their own "murderer's row" for a couple of years. Altman did not arrive in the majors until he was twenty-six, having played college baseball and then in the Negro Leagues.

"I went to Tennessee State," Altman said, "and the business manager there was a friend of Buck O'Neill. Mr. O'Neill recommended that I try out for the Kansas City Monarchs. They were primarily a barnstorming team the year I played with them because most of the real good Negro League players had signed with major league teams. Mr. O'Neill was also responsible for signing three of us at the same time with the Cubs. The others were Lou Johnson and J.C. Hartman.

"I played at Burlington, Iowa, in the minors. It wasn't too bad because Iowa was a little more liberal than a lot of states. But I did run into some problems along the way."

A native of Goldsboro, North Carolina, Altman knew all about racial prejudice. "I would get called some names in a few places, such as Quincy, Iowa, but when I got to the big leagues, I seldom heard any of that. Remember, by the time I came up (1959), it had been twelve years since Jackie Robinson got it started for us. It had died down by then.

"One thing I recall is that, initially, black players were not allowed to stay at the same hotel in St. Louis with our white Cubs teammates. It was about two years before we were able to stay there (in the Chase Park Plaza Hotel). And even then, the people from the hotel told us black players that they would let us sleep there, but they didn't want us going into the dining room.

"It was hard," Altman said. "I knew about stuff like that from growing up in the South, but it still grates on you. Things get on your mind and keep you from being relaxed, and that can affect the way you play ball. Even in dealing with teammates, you had a funny feeling ... you knew most of them actually condoned that sort of thing; they thought that separating whites and blacks was the right way to do it. We had one or two white guys, though, who would have stayed with us black players if they could have. They saw the way things were done as unfair, and they didn't like it."

Probably the most underrated of the early black players was Sam "Jet" Jethroe, a switch-hitter, who possessed blazing speed. Don Newcombe called Jethroe the fastest human being he had ever seen. In 1945, he was one of three black players — Jackie Robinson and Marvin Williams were the others — who were given a tryout by the Red Sox under pressure from a Boston city councilman. It was reported that, with only members of the club's front office in the stands, someone yelled out, "Get those niggers off the field."

The Red Sox were not interested in integrating their team, and after the token workout — Boston general manager Eddie Collins did not even attend — that was that. Despite impressing two Boston coaches, none of the three men were even contacted by anyone from the Red Sox's organization. Jethroe went back to the Negro Leagues and won his second straight batting title. In 1948, the Brooklyn Dodgers signed him and assigned him to their International League Montreal farm team after the season was under way. Jethroe batted .over .300 twice for the Royals, and in 1949, he stole 89 bases.

Rather than promote Jethroe, Brooklyn traded him to the Braves for three players and $100,000. Rickey, who was the Dodgers' general manager at the time, said it was the first time in his career that he had gotten rid of a player who was potentially better than some players he kept. Rickey also admitted that a fear by Brooklyn owners of having too many black players was a big reason the speedy out-fielder was traded.

Jethroe, who was in the Braves' 1950 opening-day lineup, led the National League in stolen bases for the first of three straight seasons and earned Rookie of the Year honors. Thirty-two at the time, though he was reported to be four years younger, Jethroe is still the oldest player to win the rookie award. Age, a poor 1952 season, and the arrival of Billy Bruton were the reasons he was sent to the minors in 1953 and then traded to Pittsburgh. Jethroe played in just two games for the Pirates in 1954 before returning to the minor leagues, where he spent five years, never again playing in the majors.

It is interesting that the first four teams — the Dodgers, Indians, Giants, and Braves — to use black players would also be the first four clubs to reap immediate and extensive rewards from the contributions of black players. The Dodgers, Giants, and Braves combined to win nine of the ten National League pennants in the 1950s. One of those three teams won every flag from 1951-59 after the Philadelphia Phillies' Whiz Kids won it to start the decade. Doby, who played thirteen years in the majors and twice led the American League in home runs, helped Cleveland win pennants in 1948 and 1954.

Roy Campanella caught in seventy-eight games for Brooklyn in

1948. He was the Dodgers' starting catcher in 1949, when Don Newcombe became his battery mate. Big Newk started thirty-one games that season, going 17-8 to win the National League Rookie of the Year Award. In 1952, the Dodgers made Joe Black the mainstay of their bullpen and recalled Sandy Amoros in late August. The next year, second baseman Jim "Junior" Gilliam joined with Black to give the Dodgers back-to-back Rookies of the Year. Beginning with Jackie Robinson, a black player was selected as the National League's top rookie eight times in thirteen years.

The Giants had five black players on their 1951 roster, but no more than four at one time. Irvin and Willie Mays, the National League Rookie of the Year, were everyday outfielders, while Hank Thompson was the starting third baseman most of the season. Mays began the season with the Giants' triple-A Minneapolis team before being called up in May. Ray Noble was the backup catcher and Artie Wilson, a little used shortstop, spent the first month of the season with the club. In May of 1951, New York manager Leo Durocher inserted Wilson as a defensive replacement. Wilson joined Irvin, Thompson, and Nobles to make the Giants the first major league team to use four black players in the same game. Ruben Gomez made 26 starts for the 1953 Giants, and he remained a member of their rotation for six years.

The Braves, who moved from Boston to Milwaukee prior to the 1953 season, added at least one black player each year from 1952-57. George Crowe played fifty-five games at first base for the 1952 Braves. Bruton replaced Jethroe in center field in 1953. That was the same year Jim Pendleton, who was traded from Brooklyn, batted .299 for Milwaukee. Hank Aaron hit 13 home runs for the 1954 Braves. Humberto Robinson was 3-1 with a 3.08 ERA in 1955, Wes Covington logged 138 at-bats in 1956 before smacking 21 and 24 homers the next two seasons, and Felix Mantilla was called up in June of the same year to provide infield backup. Left-hander Juan Pizarro started ten games and won five as a twenty-year-old member of Milwaukee's 1957 World Series championship team.

There was an unspoken quota system regarding black players during the 1950s. By the middle of the decade, three — and sometimes four — of Brooklyn's eight position players were black. Third baseman Robinson, second baseman Gilliam, and catcher Campanella were almost always in the starting lineup. They were frequently joined by left fielder Amoros, whose running catch saved the Dodgers' seventh-game victory over the Yankees in the 1955 World Series. However, Amoros did not normally start on days when Newcombe was on the mound, thereby preventing Brooklyn from having more black players than white ones on the field at the same time.

That was a private concern of the Dodgers' front office brass, who felt having too many black players would not bode well at the ticket windows. The same kind of thinking could have had something to do with the Dodgers trading Jethroe and Pendleton, the latter a shortstop standing in line behind Pee Wee Reese. Brooklyn's front office was not the only one to think that way as there seemed to be a consensus to hold the number of black players to a minimum.

What follows are partial contents of a letter from Boston Braves farm director Harry Jenkins to T.T. Baird, the president of the Kansas City Monarchs of the Negro Leagues. Dated March 9, 1951, it said, in part: "I regret that there has been a delay in answering your letter offering the contract of pitcher Jim LaMarque for $3500. The truth is we now have three colored boys at Milwaukee, and if we take another, I am fearful that the club could get top-heavy. I am certain you can recognize this is a factor to be considered. I firmly believe the pitcher would perform creditably in AAA baseball, but we simply are in no position to add him to our roster at this time."

Before he was traded by the Braves, Jethroe was sent down for the 1953 season, which was the franchise's first in Milwaukee. He was thirty-five years old, and Billy Bruton was ready to take over the club's center field job. In fact, he was already in Milwaukee, which had been the Braves' triple-A affiliate while they were located in Boston. Bruton was twenty-seven when he took the field in the season opener, a game he won with a tenth-inning home run. His black teammates that year were Pendleton and Crowe, who backed up Joe Adcock at first base.

After the season, with Aaron expected to make the Braves' big club the next year, Crowe was demoted to the minors and stayed there all of the 1954 season. When Adcock was sidelined with a broken arm the following year, Crowe proved an able fill-in. Before the next season started, Crowe was traded to Cincinnati, where he had his biggest year in 1957. He could have still helped Milwaukee, but with Aaron, Bruton, Pendleton, and Humberto Robinson on the roster, and with Covington and Mantilla on the verge of making the team, the Braves' front office might have thought there were enough black players. Ironically, a player the Braves acquired in the Crowe trade — Bob Hazle — was one of the main ingredients as they won the 1957 National League pennant and the World Series.

Both of the 1954 World Series teams had four black players. Mays and Irvin were in the New York outfield, and Thompson was at third base. Gomez, after winning 17 games during the regular season, notched a victory in the Series as the Giants swept Cleveland in four games. Doby and Al Smith started in the Indians' outfield, where Dave Pope played in a reserve role. Dave Hoskins was a member of their pitching staff.

The "black quota" notion disappeared from the majors in the 1960s. Anxiety over percentages was over-ridden by the desire to put the best players on the field, and an increasing number of the best players were black. The American League's slow start in signing black players was still having a noticeable effect when the decade opened, as a total of only twenty-two blacks were used by the league's eight teams in 1960, while sixty-five blacks played for National League clubs the same year. In 1969, however, seventy-five blacks played for the American League teams, and 101 blacks appeared in games for clubs in the National League. There were twelve teams in each league by then, but an increase of more than one hundred percent was substantial.

Equally telling is a look at starting lineups in the middle of the decade. In 1964, thirty-eight black players were starters on a regular basis in the National League and sixteen in the American League. Almost half of the black National League starters had earned star status, and a dozen of those were acknowledged superstars. The San Francisco Giants and Los Angeles Dodgers both started six blacks most of the time, with the Cincinnati Reds, Philadelphia Phillies, and the St. Louis Cardinals starting four apiece. The Chicago White Sox and Minnesota Twins had the most black regular starters in the American League with three each. The New York Yankees, Boston

Red Sox, Cleveland Indians, Kansas City A's, Washington Senators, and Baltimore Orioles all had just one. (Starters refer to the eight position players, and not pitchers.)

It was not until September 1, 1971, that a major league baseball team started a lineup consisting of all black players. On that day, at Pittsburgh's Three Rivers Stadium, Pirates manager Danny Murtaugh penciled the following names onto his lineup card to face the Philadelphia Phillies:

Rennie Stennett 2B
Gene Clines CF
Roberto Clemente RF
Willie Stargell LF
Manny Sanguillen C
Dave Cash 3B
Al Oliver 1B
Jackie Hernandez SS
Dock Ellis P

Fourteen black players helped the Pirates to win the National League pennant and the World Series title that season — twenty-four years after Jackie Robinson's historic first major league game.

And, while that Pittsburgh lineup may have provided a landmark, nobody was counting black stars in the major leagues any more. They became commonplace in the 1960s.

Chapter 13
Visiting the Babe's House

Entering "fantasy land" that was Yankee Stadium

I am not crazy about the new Yankee Stadium. I have not been there, and everything that I have read about it is complimentary. My daughter has seen a game there, and she raves about it. I guess it's just that I never understood the reason for building the new place. Like many followers of baseball, I did not know what was so awfully wrong with the old one. Why would anyone mess with such tradition unless the stadium was falling apart, and it wasn't. Keep in mind that Fenway Park and Wrigley Field are both older than the original Yankee Stadium. I'm sure I was not the only person to view as sacrilege the moving of the monuments (Babe Ruth, Lou Gehrig, Joe DiMaggio, Mickey Mantle, Miller Huggins) across the street to the shiny new structure the Pinstripes started calling home in 2009.

The Yankee Stadium, the House that Ruth built, was one of the true shrines in baseball, as are Fenway and Wrigley. I can't imagine the ghosts of the Babe, the Iron Horse, the Clipper, and the Mick bothering to haunt the Yanks' fancy new digs with the home run wind tunnel in right field. They are probably insulted.

Visiting the Babe's House was always a treat for baseball fans. It didn't matter whether they were Yankee fans. Going there, being there, for a baseball fan was kind of like any American seeing the Lincoln Memorial and Washington Monument while in the nation's capital. It was a have-to-see part of baseball history.

I attended two games in Yankee Stadium. One a few years before it closed. The other when I was fifteen years old.

I was part of a group of Boy Scouts that took a two-week bus trip to Montreal, Canada. Up there, some of us made a long, tortuous canoe expedition on a rough, rapid-raged river. Sticking it out and making it to the finish remains one of my proudest accomplishments, not because it required any particular skill, but because it was difficult and took a lot of determination. At night, we slept out in the open, not in a tent, under a sky that seemed clearer and stars that glowed brighter than the sky and stars back in North Carolina.

The whole trip was a great experience, but the highlights for me were seeing a game in Yankee Stadium and spending time at the Baseball Hall of Fame in Cooperstown, New York.

It was 1961, and it had been three years since I had been to a big league ball game. The prospect of just seeing another one was exciting enough, but knowing I was going to actually sit in the stands and watch a game at Yankee Stadium had me counting the hours until it happened. I could not wait.

We were going to see the Yankees play the Chicago White Sox, and although I was hoping New York would lose, I was pulling for Roger Maris and Mickey Mantle to hit home runs. Known as the M&M

Boys, they had hit a bunch of homers to that point of the season.

Much had been written about the possibility that one, or both, of the outfielders would break Babe Ruth's 1927 record of hitting 60 home runs in one season. There were magazine stories about the friendly competition between two teammates, and some of those stories suggested the rivalry was less than friendly. I chose to believe Mantle and Maris, although naturally competitive, were supportive of each other, and I think evidence over the years has proven that to be true.

Mantle jumped to a fast start, hitting seven homers in April, while Maris blasted 11 in May and 15 in June. At the end of July, Maris had 40 home runs and Mantle had 39. Our group of Scouts was in Yankee Stadium on August 17, 1961, for an afternoon game. Maris had 48 home runs after hitting a pair off of White Sox left-hander Billy Pierce the previous day. That gave Maris 112 runs batted in. Mantle had not homered since August 13, when he hit number 45.

I remember thinking that the odds were in favor of Mantle hitting a home run because he had not done so in four days. I figured the chances were also good that Maris would homer because he was hot. It might have been wishful thinking, but I turned contrasting situations into positive calculating for each slugger.

When our bus was approaching New York City, everyone was looking out the windows at the captivating skyline. As we were driving past the towering skyscrapers, we gawked at buildings taller than most of us had ever seen. It was menacing the way they hulked over us. The skyscrapers seemed to stretch through the clouds. Many of us were North Carolina country boys who may have seen pictures of New York City's gigantic buildings, but we were unprepared for how imposing they would be when viewed in person.

Upon entering Yankee Stadium, I was dazzled by all of the souvenirs available. The thing that struck me the most was a replica Yankee batting helmet. I had always loved the way baseball teams' helmets looked. The ones on sale were plastic and were to be worn for fun; they weren't the protective type players used in games. One of those babies cost five dollars, much more than I had to spend. More than half of our trip was ahead of us, and I had to ration my money. Even though I was not a fan of the Yankees, I have always liked their caps.

They have a classic simplistic look, extremely dark blue with an NY (the Y over the N) in front. I thought about buying a cap for three dollars, but decided that was also too much. Plus, I did not want to wear a Yankees cap. I walked from one souvenir stand to another, seeing if one might offer something the others did not have, something I might like and could afford.

I finally bought a scorecard for a quarter. I figured if I kept up with what every batter did during the game, my record of what took place that day would be the best memento of all. And cheap, too. Several years ago, when I found it in the attic, that folded two-page scorecard was torn through the middle, and the corners were jagged. I had not thought to put it into anything for protection and preservation, and my record of a big day at Yankee Stadium was falling apart. I'm glad I copied down my notations, allowing me to reconstruct the game I saw.

An hour or so before game time, a Yankee Stadium usher led our group to the center field bleachers, where we were able to look down upon the famous monuments which sat right on the playing field. At that time, there were just three monuments. They honored Miller Huggins, Lou Gehrig, and Babe Ruth.

Huggins, a Hall of Fame manager who took the Yankees to six American League pennants and three World Series titles, died late in the 1929 season. Three years later, the team dedicated a monument to him, and it was erected on the ground in front of the flag pole, which was 450 feet from home plate. Following the deaths of Gehrig and Ruth, monuments were added in 1941 and 1949, respectively, to commemorate the two legendary New York stars. Those were the monuments I saw.

Over the years, batted balls sometimes made their way to the hallowed ground where the monuments sat. It was reported that, on one such occasion, Yankees manager Casey Stengel comically shouted toward the field where his outfielder was fumbling with the ball, "Ruth, Gehrig, Huggins, somebody … get that ball back to the infield."

In 1970, Yankee stadium was remodeled, and the three monuments were moved off of the playing field to an enclosed area behind the fence in left-center field. The area between the two bullpens came to be known as "Monument Park." Two more monuments were erected to honor super center fielders: one in 1996, a year after the death of Mickey Mantle, the other in 1999, a month after the death of Joe DiMaggio. The monuments, as well as plaques honoring several other Yankee stars, were moved to the new Yankee Stadium.

I remember smiling to myself as I gazed at the three monuments. I was thinking how, just a few years earlier, I had thought that the monuments were headstones and that Miller Huggins, Lou Gehrig, and Babe Ruth were buried under the Yankee Stadium turf.

New York right-hander Bill Stafford set the White Sox down in order in the top of the first inning. Second baseman Bobby Richardson led off with a single for the Yankees. After Tony Kubek flied to deep right field and Maris struck out, Mantle, a switch-hitter batting right-handed, got hold of a pitch from lefty Frank Bauman and gave it a ride. The ball was hit to straightaway center field, chasing Jim Landis to the wall. He ran out of room, and the drive bounced high off the fence.

Mantle, who possessed blistering speed before hurting a knee early in his major league career, could still run faster than most players. Watching him hit the inside corner of the bag at first base and then dash to third for a stand-up triple, I could only imagine a speedier Mantle. He looked like a blur to me. The RBI was the 105th for the popular center fielder, and the Yankees led, 1-0.

In the third inning, Maris grounded out to shortstop Luis Aparicio, and Mantle walked. The Yankees added three runs in the fourth. Hector Lopez reached on an error by Aparicio and Clete Boyer walked. After Stafford struck out, Richardson singled Lopez home and Boyer also came around to score when White Sox left fielder Minnie Minoso let the ball get through him. Kubek's double plated Richardson. Maris and Mantle both grounded out. New York led, 4-0.

Ever since we found out that Yankee Stadium was one of the destinations on our trip, a few of us Scouts who were good friends had been talking about getting a foul ball. We were not thinking about the thousands of people who would be in the stands with us. We were not thinking about the slim chance that a foul would even be hit in our direction. As the game moved along, not a single foul ball had come remotely close to us. Whenever a batter fouled one into the crowd, and we could see who came up with the ball, we would talk about how lucky that person was. In the fifth inning, White Sox right fielder Floyd Robinson hit a high fly which appeared to be headed right at us. It dropped about a dozen rows in front of us, bounded high off of the concrete walkway, and settled into the hands of a lady. She was not wearing a glove and did not act very eager at all. The ball simply found her. We spent the next two innings asking why that couldn't have been us.

The Yanks made it 5-0 in the sixth. Richardson and Kubek singled, Richardson moving to third base when Maris forced Kubek at second. Mantle bounced out to third as Richardson scored, giving Mantle his 106th run batted in.

Chicago rallied for three runs in the ninth, but came up short when New York manager Ralph Houk waved in relief ace Luis Arroyo from the bullpen. The stocky southpaw closed out the Yankees' 5-3 win to earn his 23rd save. I recalled that I had seen Arroyo at Forbes Field in Pittsburgh four years earlier, and he was pitching poorly for a poor Pirates team. Shows what a difference it makes to have a strong supporting cast.

I was pulling hard for the White Sox to tie the score and send the game into extra innings. It wasn't just that I was cheering for them to beat the Yankees; I did not want the game to end. When it did, after what was a very fast two and a half hours, I felt a surge of disappointment. It was like air leaving a balloon. I had a great time, but the day I had looked forward to for so long and with so much anticipation was over.

Maris went 0-for-4, Mantle 1-for-3 with a walk and two RBI. The highlight was watching Mantle fly from home to third on his smash to center field. That mental video is running as I write this.

I had read so much about Mickey Mantle and the electricity he generated everywhere he went. That feeling was certainly evident to me that August afternoon in Yankee Stadium. Whenever Mantle walked into the on-deck circle, the crowd noticed and began to stir. When he made his way to the batter's box, I sensed that all of the 25,532 people on hand had grown suddenly more attentive, feeling that something spectacular might happen. And, the truth was that Mantle's sheer presence was special. The triple and two runs he batted in were gravy.

Maris did break Ruth's record that season. He hit 61 home runs and won his second straight Most Valuable Player award. Mantle finished with 54 homers. Although I wished I could have seen at least one of the 115 homers the M&M Boys combined to clout in 1961, I was thrilled just to have been in Yankee Stadium, to have seen a game played there. There was no one among our busload of Boy Scouts and adult leaders who got a bigger kick out of that afternoon than I did.

Chapter 14
A Baggy Old Uniform

Throwaway rags become cherished threads

I attended Seventy-First High School. The name was derived from a Cumberland County community, a township named by Scottish immigrants who were descendents of the Seventy-First Regiment of the Scottish Highlanders. My mother had graduated from the same high school, and when I began there in the ninth grade, Seventy-First was located smack-dab in the middle of farm land. It was a country school. Today, things have changed dramatically as the land has been developed, businesses have sprung up, and the school, one of the largest in our county, is not considered so rural.

The Seventy-First baseball coach was Dwight Miller. A prisoner of war during World War II, Mr. Miller was one of the finest people I have ever known. At one time or another, he coached just about every sport in which Seventy-First fielded a team.

It was early February of my sophomore year when Mr. Miller announced over the intercom that varsity baseball tryouts would begin the following Monday. I was excited and could hardly wait. Thirty-six boys were competing for fourteen roster spots, but in reality, twenty-six for vying for four. Ten players were returning from a team which had gone 4-10. My hopes were not brightened by the fact that two outstanding juniors were added to the mix, both having recently moved into the school district when their fathers were stationed at Fort Bragg.

Normally, freshmen were not selected on varsity teams, but there were exceptions now and then. Two such exceptions appeared certain to make the baseball team. One was my cousin, Samuel Guy, a bull-like strong boy who could hit a ball a long way and run very fast to boot. He was a pretty good catcher and a better outfielder. The other freshman standout was a pitcher, tall and talented, who looked as if he might be one of the team's starting hurlers.

Sure enough, both of their names were on the list Mr. Miller tacked to the gymnasium door. Mine was not. I was heartbroken. And, although I knew deep down that I was probably not one of the best fourteen players, I was still disappointed. I say "probably" because I thought I was at least as good as a couple of guys who made it. But they were seniors, and they had been on the team the year before. I understood about that.

I was attempting to swallow the king-sized lump in my throat, while at the same time trying to make myself invisible because I felt warm water in my eyes, when Mr. Miller materialized out of nowhere. Putting an arm around my shoulders and walking me away from the crowd of boys whose jubilance made it obvious they had made the team, he tried to console me. He told me that he knew it was unlikely anyone wanted to make that team more than I did.

He said that I reminded him of himself when he was in high school — not very strong physically, extremely strong fundamentally, and possessing a tremendous amount of desire. Mr. Miller said that made him want to keep me all the more. But, he said, that would not have been fair to fourteen boys he felt were better than me. I nodded, unable, because of the tears in my eyes and the lump in my throat, to do anything else. He patted me on the back, started to say something else, and then turned and walked away.

Following a week of tryouts, there were still two weeks before the high school baseball season opened. I asked Samuel every day how practice was going, and he tried not to sound too enthusiastic because he knew how hard it was for me, not being on the team. He was kind enough not to go into great detail about who was doing what, and he never bragged about making the team despite being just a freshman. I did not have the heart to stay after school and watch the team practice. That would have been too painful.

It was the Tuesday before our team was scheduled to play its first game on a Friday. I was in Latin class, when a knock came at the door, and my teacher called to me, "Mr. Miller needs to see you right away. And hurry back because we are working some on conjugation today, and no one can afford to miss much of that."

I thought I knew what Mr. Miller wanted. He had asked me the previous day if I knew how to keep a baseball scorebook, and I told him I did. I figured he was looking for a scorekeeper and was going to ask me if I wanted the job. I had already decided my answer would be no. For two reasons: I wanted to be a player, not a scorekeeper, and my chores at home required quite a bit of time. Getting home right after school allowed me time to get them done and also finish my homework and still get to bed at a reasonable hour. Of course, had I made the team, missing some sleep would not have mattered.

When I arrived at Mr. Miller's classroom, he took me back to the little area behind a partition where coats were hung. Smiling broadly and saying he may have some good news for me, he bent over, reached down, and pulled something from a brown paper bag. It was an ancient baseball uniform, rumpled and faded and somewhat threadbare. And it was huge. Mr. Miller explained that he was going through an old equipment trunk, and he found the uniform. He said he knew it was pretty old and way too big for me, but that if I didn't mind wearing it and if my mother could take it up enough so that it wouldn't fall off of me, I was welcome to it.

I stupidly asked why he was giving me the uniform. Did he want me to coach first base or something? Mr. Miller laughed and said, no, he wanted me to be a member of the baseball team. He wanted me to practice and keep improving, and he said that maybe he could get me into a game or two.

It sounded like sympathy to me, but I never was opposed to a little sympathy now and then, so I paused for about half a second, then I jumped up and down, yelling that of course I wanted to be on the team. Grinning as he asked me to calm down and be a bit quieter, Mr. Miller reminded me that the old jersey and pants he gave me might fall apart when my mother took a needle and thread to them and that she might not be able to alter it so I could even wear it. I assured him that she could fix it up, that it would be just fine.

And so it was that my high school baseball career began. I practiced with the team the next day, and I was in uniform, such as it was, for the opening game. Not before Mother did a powerful amount of work, though. Because the uniform had yellowed over the years, she had to bleach it back to white. It practically disintegrated in two places where she tried to rip seams and sew it back together, so she had to find some old white fabric and attach it beneath the surface. She was a wizard. When she was finished patching, cutting, sewing, and scrubbing, that uniform looked entirely different. Mr. Miller did a double-take when he saw it on me. The uniform was only one size too big when it had been three. It was a little baggy, but that was okay. The important things were that I could wear it and that it looked pretty much like my teammates' uniforms.

There was no number on the back of the shirt. I had always kind of liked thirteen, and no one else on our team had it. Mr. Miller said that could be my number if I didn't think it would be unlucky, so Mother bought a red one and three, sewed them on the jersey, and I wore it proudly.

I did not play in the first game or the second or the third. Not that I expected to; after all, just practicing with the team and suiting up for games were big deals for me. I was working out at second base and at third, taking as many grounders as anyone else, and I was getting my allotment of swings in batting practice. One thing was different, though. Mr. Miller directed me to bunt more balls than anyone else. The truth is, I was a better bunter than hitter, and that was one thing I did better than anyone on the team.

In the fourth game, our shortstop was having an awful day. A very talented fielder who tried too hard and was always nervous, he had an awful day every time we played. He bobbled one ground ball after another, and when he did field one cleanly, he often made a bad throw. On this particular afternoon, he had already made three errors before committing two on one play in the fifth inning. His head was hanging as low as his confidence level, and he let an easy roller go right through his legs. Three errors in one inning and six for the game.

Mr. Miller just shook his head, but did not embarrass the boy further by taking him out in the middle of the inning. When our team came in to bat, the coach announced that, when we went back out in the field, our third baseman would move to shortstop and Mumau would go in at third. Then he nodded at me and told me to throw with someone and get loose.

I played the last two innings, catching an easy foul pop-up in my only chance in the field, and hitting a soft bouncer to the second baseman in my first varsity at-bat. We got trounced, and although I knew better than to show it, I was extremely happy just to have played.

That game was on a Friday, and when we practiced on Monday, Mr. Miller surprisingly sent me to third base to take infield with the first team. The boy who had been our third baseman remained at short. I kind of felt bad for the benched shortstop, a senior, whose spirits had been crushed by his own misplays. But I was glad for the chance, and I really couldn't believe it was happening.

Our next game was the following day, a Tuesday, and we were at home. I was in the starting lineup, playing third base and batting eighth. Nothing was hit my way in the first few innings. Then a right-handed batter slapped a routine two-hopper right at me. I reached for the ball, let it hit off the end of my glove, groped for it, and dropped it. An error on my first ground ball. I felt my face turning a dark shade of red. I was burning with humiliation. I looked at Mr. Miller on the bench and expected to see him looking away in disgust. Instead, he stood up, clapped his hands, and shouted that I had my jitters out of the way, and I would be fine.

I walked my first time at bat, sacrificed a runner to second the next trip to the plate, and lined out sharply to the shortstop. The highlight came in the last inning. We led by two runs, and the visiting team had a runner on second with one out. The batter hit a smash down the third-base line between me and the bag. I backhanded it behind the base and had my right foot in foul territory when I rifled a throw to first that just nipped the batter. The next guy made an out, and we had won. I had contributed to that win, and when my teammates slapped me on the back and congratulated me on my defensive play, I felt I was truly a part of the team.

The next game saw me get my first base hit, a solid line drive to right field. I got a blooper to left and a bunt single the game after that, and I knocked in the go-ahead run with a hard single to center the game after that. After six games as a starter, I was batting over .300, had struck out only twice, and I was playing good defense. We would win a game and then lose one, unable to string a series of victories together because our pitching was not the greatest.

Personally, the season was going well when the strangest thing happened. I should say that I did the strangest thing. Our team was batting with a two-run lead, and it was the fifth inning. With a runner on first and no outs, Mr. Miller, looking for insurance, gave me the bunt sign. I fouled the first pitch back, and I quickly glanced down to the third-base coach's box, where Mr. Miller appeared to be disgusted. That was my take on his expression, anyway. The next four pitches were balls, and I trotted to first with a walk, the runner on first moving to second. Obviously, our situation was better than if I had gotten the bunt down. But I felt my coach was disappointed in me, that I had somehow let him down. I thought that he believed I should always be able to put a bunt into fair territory because, after all, that was my strength offensively.

We won the ball game, but I went home terribly upset with myself. When I explained my emotions to my daddy, he said that it didn't make sense for me to feel the way I did, that the runner had advanced, plus I had reached base, and so there was no way my coach would be disappointed in me. For some reason, I could not accept that. I felt I had let Mr. Miller down, and I could not bear doing that, so I decided I would just quit the team.

We played again the next day, and when I walked into the house after riding the bus from school, my mother's face showed her astonishment. She was getting ready to drive to the game, and she wanted to know if it had been postponed. I told her it had not, that I had decided not to play any more because I had failed at what I was supposed to do best and had let my coach down in the process. Mother was furious. She informed me, and not mildly, that I was not going to quit. She said my reason for even considering it was a lousy one and that, no matter what, I was going to finish what I started.

I grew angry, my pride was hurt, and tears welled up in my eyes. But I did as I was told, and I put on my uniform. By the time we arrived at the ball field, my eyes were red and I was wishing I could be anywhere but where I was. The walk from our car to the Seventy-First bench seemed like miles, and I felt like hundreds of eyes were zooming in on me and my tear-stained face.

I sneaked down to the very end of the bench, hoping my coach wouldn't notice, but as I sat down, Mr. Miller leaned forward and eyed me from the other end. I just knew he was going to ball me out in front of the team and everybody seated and standing behind our bench. But he didn't. He didn't say a word. The game had just started, and Mr. Miller didn't turn his head in my direction again. Until the third inning, when he stood up, walked down to where I sat with my head in my hands, and he said, "Thad, get loose. You're going in at third base when we go back out in the field."

That was it. He never asked me why I showed up after the game had started, never punished me for being late. I realized that was because of his maturity and because of his experience working with youngsters. Even from as far away as he was sitting, it must have been evident from my red eyes that something was wrong. And, he figured, whatever it was might be helped by my getting out there and playing some baseball. He was right.

I have no idea how many times I have told that story over the years. I recounted it more than once with Mr. Miller, and I always told him how much I appreciated the way he treated me.

Seventy-First won eight games and lost eight that season. I batted .316, and after butchering that first ground ball hit to me, I did not make another error of any kind. All of my hits were singles. I bunted for a base hit twice and had three sacrifice bunts.

When I turned in that old, baggy uniform to Mr. Miller after the season, he said it was time to take it out of commission. He said if I wanted to keep it, I could. I carried it home, and my mother wrapped the uniform in a plastic bag and told me to put it in the cedar chest in our attic. Years later, while cleaning out that chest, I opened the bag and removed the uniform. Only it wasn't a uniform any more. It fell to pieces, practically disintegrating. I pulled the number thirteen off the tatters that remained of the jersey, and I threw the bag of shreds into the trash.

The following year, students in grades nine through twelve moved into a new building across the road, leaving creaky, antiquated Seventy-First School for shiny, modern Seventy-First High School. I started at second base my junior season, one which was just mediocre for me and the team. My senior year, we got a new coach, brand-new uniforms, and two boxes of new bats.

Ted Chappell, an outstanding coach and an even better person, ordered two dozen bats, Louisville Sluggers and Adirondacks, and he did not open the boxes until the first practice after the last cut had been made. Among those twenty-four bats were two Vada Pinson Adirondack models. They were thirty-four and one-half inches long and weighed thirty ounces. They were long, light, and perfectly balanced, with a handle that was neither too thin nor too thick. I used a Pinson model all season, led the team in batting average, and attributed much of my success to that bat.

Seventy-First was loaded with talent that season, and we had a tremendous team. We made it all the way to the state semifinals. I played first base, hit better than I ever had in my life, and enjoyed a strong overall season. I came through with some big hits and made a few outstanding defensive plays along the way. Anyone would have been happy to end a career with a season filled with team and individual success.

And I have certainly always remembered that. But not as vividly and as fondly as I remember that first uniform and that first season.

Chapter 15
A Place to Play

Playing semi-pro baseball in a new setting

The Fayetteville Cardinals had been an all-black semi-pro baseball team since being formed in the 1950s. Up until a couple of years earlier, when two white soldiers tried out and were kept on the club. I had heard about the Cardinals, but I had never seen them play. Following graduation from high school in June of 1964, I took a summer job at a fast-food hamburger place. I wanted to play baseball, but there was no recreation league for anyone my age. Then, one day, I read in the sports section of our newspaper that the Fayetteville Cardinals were holding tryouts and that anyone seventeen years of age and older was welcome.

The team was run by a man named Willie Smith. He raised money for uniforms and equipment, scheduled games with any opposition he could find within a reasonable distance, and managed the team.

The tryouts were quite an experience. My high school, like all of the others in our county, was still segregated at that time, as were all of the city's recreation leagues. So I had never played with or against a black person. My introduction to integration was, ironically, as a member of the minority. The Fayetteville Cardinals, after inviting anyone interested to go out for the team, had included two white players on their roster each of the previous two seasons. I had to admit I was a little apprehensive simply because I did not know what to expect.

As soon as I walked onto the ball field, I knew in a very small way what it felt like to be one of the "other fellows". There were five white guys trying out, and three of us made the cut. From the first minute all the way through every inning I played in four seasons with the Cardinals, everyone was extremely nice. The main thing — what I realized black people always wanted — was that those guys treated us white fellows just like they treated each other. The razzing, the encouragement, the criticism … it was the same for everybody.

We played our games at Jim Hodges Park, which was located outside of Fayetteville among a patch of trees just off of Highway 301 South. A couple of hundred yards from the ball diamond was an old church attended by black people. Most of the games began on Sunday afternoons at three o'clock. Players arrived at 1:30, and a half hour or so after we had started throwing and taking ground balls, folks came streaming out of the small sanctuary. Many of the people migrated over to the ball field. Women took off their Sunday hats and men removed suit coats and loosened ties. They bought hot dogs and soft drinks, and they settled onto the rusty metal bleachers to cheer on their Cardinals.

One of the two other white players was a catcher who had graduated from a local high school the previous year. The second was a soldier who was stationed at Fort Bragg and who had played shortstop for two years in the minor leagues.

Baseball with the Cardinals was quite an adventure. Almost all of our games were played on Saturday nights and Sunday afternoons. We played a few games on week nights, a handful of Friday night games, and a July Fourth doubleheader. Our opponents included teams with former major leaguers, small-town teams made up of mill workers, and a prison team. The latter traveled to our field forty miles on a bus, and I remember the team brought an armed guard. He carried a rifle, and he walked back and forth behind the team's bench. The bench was located down the third-base line, and that day, I was playing third. The guy with the gun was very distracting, and I kept hoping none of those prisoners would bolt and decide to run past me.

The prison team's pitcher threw a knuckleball, a really good knuckler that danced all over the place. He said his name was Boyce Wilhelm, and he claimed to be a cousin of Hoyt Wilhelm, a North Carolina-born Hall of Fame pitcher who threw one of the best knuckleballs ever. I never did check out whether that was true, but Boyce's knuckleball sure looked like it could have been related to Hoyt's.

One day, we were playing at home, and I had brought a teen-aged boy with me to the game. Freddy Proctor was a close friend, and he loved baseball. Before the game started, Willie Smith asked Freddy if he would work the scoreboard. It was located on the wall in right field. Freddy sat on a stool in foul territory, and he hung the appropriate number after each half inning.

Weeds had grown up pretty high several feet in front of the fence, and along about the third inning, something moved in those weeds. Then a man sat up and let out a long, loud, gut-wrenching moan, bringing everything to a standstill. Everything but Freddy, that is. He came dashing to our bench, eyes wide, as if he had seen a ghost. In fact, that is exactly what he thought he had seen. It turned out the man was sleeping off a rough Saturday night, and no one had noticed him because the weeds were so thick. Freddy's scoreboard duties were finished. He sat in the stands behind our bench for the rest of the game and kept one eye on the area in front of the scoreboard.

Some other strange and amusing things happened at Jim Hodges Park. The strangest and most amusing occurred in a game in which the opposing pitcher had a no-hitter going. We were batting in the bottom of the eighth when an extremely disturbing noise reverberated from left field. The fence out there was comprised of several sheets of silver-colored metal which were propped against one another and not really connected. The clatter everyone heard came from something banging against that section of fence. After a few more pitches, we saw what that something was. The BAM! was repeated, a piece of the metal fell to the ground, and a white horse appeared. On it was someone dressed like a knight from the days of King Arthur.

The knight charged toward the infield, headed for home plate, and galloped around the bases, yelling something no one could understand as he left the same way he came in. Several players propped the metal fence back up, and the game resumed. The opposing pitcher, visibly shaken, walked the next two batters and then gave up three hits in a row. After the game, Cardinal players tried to convince the pitcher that the knight and white horse were not part of a ploy routinely used to upset visiting hurlers.

By this time, I had learned the difference between chewing tobacco and pipe tobacco. I occasionally chewed during games, and I had found a way to prevent pieces of tobacco from drifting toward the back of my mouth and down my throat. Before a game started, I would chew four pieces of bubble gum, remove it from my mouth, and stretch it out. I then stuck a sizeable amount of Red Man right in the middle of my pink blanket, folded the gum around the tobacco, and crammed the large wad into the back of my jaw. The gum held everything together.

One day, while playing third base, my chew worked its way too far toward the back of my mouth, moving from my jaw to an area between a wisdom tooth and my throat. I stuck a finger into my mouth, trying to dislodge the mass, but that was to no avail. The game was going on, the Cardinals were out in the field, and I would have been too embarrassed to call time out so I could re-arrange my chaw. Tobacco juice began trickling down my throat, and I started to see two of everything. I was hoping I would not have to make a fielding play. If I did, I was hoping I could choose the correct ball from the two I was seeing.

As luck would have it, a ball was sharply grounded toward the hole between third and shortstop. I dove to my left and made a nice stop, but instead of springing to my feet and throwing to first, I just laid there. Very still. My teammates ran onto the field to see what was wrong. They told me later that when they rolled me over, my face was a pale shade of green. I had swallowed my chew of tobacco. I was so sick that I had to leave the game. I gave the rest of my bag of Red

Man to a teammate, and I switched to good old bubble gum.

Cardinals general manager, manager, and traveling secretary Willie Smith was one of the nicest men I have ever met. He loved baseball, he loved people, and he loved life. He always wore a pair of black slacks, a short-sleeved white shirt, black wingtip shoes, and a straw hat with a short brim and a black band. He had a pencil-thin mustache and laughing eyes that went perfectly with his broad smile, something else he always wore. What a great guy to be around.

Players who had been with the Cardinals for several years told me that Willie would hold a serious team meeting after a game late every season. They snickered when they told me and said the annual meeting was always a real gem. Sure enough, in early August, it happened. We had split a doubleheader, and everyone was dog tired following more than six hours of baseball in 100-degree heat and 99 percent humidity. Sunday doubleheaders started at one o'clock, or as close to the hour as the umpires could get to Jim Hodges Park, and there was a half-hour break between games.

The sun was going down. Shadows had covered the entire ball field, and by the time all of the equipment was bagged, it was after eight o'clock. Willie had notified us of the meeting when we huddled before the first game, and he reminded us several times during the day to stick around after the second game ended. We were sitting on the ground or leaning against trees, eating hot dogs and drinking Pepsis, when Willie slowly walked up and stood in the middle of his players. He was holding a fistful of cash, and he nervously thumbed the green bills like a deck of cards as he cleared his throat to speak. He took off his hat and held it in the same hand as the money, while pulling a red handkerchief out of his back pocket and mopping his forehead.

Replacing his hat and gripping the stack of bills with both hands, as if the weight was too much for one, Willie said, "Gentlemen, I told you before the season started that I would try to help you out with your gas money and maybe add a few dollars extra when I could. That's what this money is for. Now, I know it's not much — it's the gate from today, and I knew this would be our best draw of the summer — but maybe it will help some. I know you boys have had to shell out to play for the Cardinals, and I wish it didn't have to be that way. What I really wish is that our crowds were big enough so I could pay each one of you fifty dollars a game. But it's not that way. So, here is twenty-five dollars apiece. It's the best I can do."

With that, he walked around to each of us and handed us bills that added up to twenty-five dollars. We started heading toward our cars when Willie said, "I just want you to know that it takes a lot of money to run a ball club. I have to pay the umpires, and you can see all the baseballs we need for every game. Bats are expensive, and they keep breaking. Every year, I have to replace some uniforms that wear out, and I buy your hats so you don't have to. We make a little bit off of concessions, but not much. I'm hoping I don't have to take out a loan to pay off all my expenses for this season. But if I do, I do. The main thing is that you boys have a chance to play ball. That the Cardinals' legacy continues. I want to thank you all."

A pitcher, who was forty-three years old and had been with the Cardinals longer than anybody, walked over to Willie and handed him his money. When he turned back toward the rest of us, he said, almost too low to be heard, "Just like last year … just like every other year." He was smiling as he said it, and so was everyone else as we all returned our twenty-five dollars. It was part of the team's annual rites, Willie giving his players money, and his players giving it back.

I felt I should have paid Willie for the opportunity. The Fayetteville Cardinals gave me a chance to play the game I loved. I played with them three more summers. There were new teammates every year, and we were never much better than a .500 club. The experiences were unforgettable, as were most of the guys I played with and folks I met who attended many of our home games.

Jim Hodges Park, with its wobbly fences, rickety bleachers, and sun-baked benches, was no baseball cathedral. Except to us Cardinals. It was a marvelous playground for a college boy salivating for a place to play some baseball. I can picture the ball park clearly. Just as clearly, I can see Willie Smith, hands jammed into the pockets of those black slacks, grinning — not because of the illustrious team he put on the field, but just because there was a team out there. And because he was a part of baseball.

I felt the same way.

Chapter 16
Meeting Mr. Clemente

Finding royalty in a locker
room with the great Roberto

In the early-morning hours of Saturday, August 1, 1970, I drove to Atlanta with my daddy and a friend. We were going to attend the Braves' games with Pittsburgh that afternoon and the next day.

I was working at *The Fayetteville Observer*, and I had contacted the Braves media relations director, who graciously agreed to leave me a working press pass and two complimentary tickets for both games at Fulton County Stadium. I planned to interview a few players, particularly Roberto Clemente.

I was concerned whether I would even have an opportunity to talk with Clemente. He had been hit by a pitch from Larry Dierker of the Houston Astros six days earlier and had not been in the Pirates' lineup since. There was an encouraging sign, though, as Clemente had appeared in the previous night's game as a pinch-runner.

Game time on Saturday was 3:10 in the afternoon, but the three of us were at the gates of Atlanta Fulton County Stadium when they opened two hours before that. We wanted to watch batting practice and soak up everything we could. We even got a kick out of watching the ground crew prepare the field.

I went to the Pirates' locker room (members of the press are allowed access to major league clubhouses for a certain period before games as well as after they have ended). I saw the Pittsburgh lineup for the day posted, and I was disappointed that Clemente was not in it. I figured he would likely be in the trainer's room for some kind of treatment and, therefore, not available for reporters.

But I was wrong. As I walked among the lockers of the Pirates' players, there was Clemente, standing in front of his cubicle. He wore his uniform pants, black stirrups with the gold rings, and a baseball undershirt — white with long black sleeves. His uniform shirt with number 21 on the back hung on the locker door.

I must admit that I was plenty nervous as I walked toward the man known in Pittsburgh as The Great One. I almost wished he would disappear into the trainer's room so that I would have an excuse for not speaking with him. I had looked forward to this moment so much, and now that it had arrived, I wasn't sure if I would be able to talk.

When I introduced myself, saying I was from Fayetteville, North Carolina, Clemente stuck out his right hand, smiled, and said, "Hey, I'm from Carolina also." (He was born in Carolina, Puerto Rico.) The ice was broken. I told him I had been a fan of his for a long time and that my daddy had taken me to see him play his first few years in the majors. I explained that I wanted to talk to him about his career and about how he had often been misunderstood by the media and, as a result, by fans.

By way of background, let me point out that Roberto Clemente was a very proud and a very sensitive man. He was passionate about being one of the best baseball players of all time and about representing his country. He wanted to show the world what a fine person and athlete his home country had produced.

For at least a half century, much has been written and said about athletes — especially professional athletes — "playing hurt", performing in spite of injuries because that is what they are paid to do. Athletes who sit out with ailments perceived by the press and public to be minor have often been maligned.

Clemente was one such athlete. He had been called many things, among them a hypochondriac and complainer, in sports columns. In addition, some writers had even made fun of his use of the English language by writing words exactly as Clemente said them, making him look foolish in the process.

Anyone spending even a few minutes in conversation with Roberto Clemente would realize immediately that he was quite intelligent and articulate. Learning a new language is never easy, especially when done on the fly. His first few years in the major leagues were also his first few years in the United States, and he was having to learn to speak English while being interviewed by people who wrote his words down for the public's digestion and inspection.

Clemente asked me again which newspaper I worked for, and he seemed glad that it was one printed in North Carolina and not New York City or Chicago. He said that I sounded sincere about wanting to tell his side of the story in regard to injuries. I had let him know that I was quite familiar with all of his major league accomplishments, and that made him happy. He was proud of what he had done.

So, Roberto Clemente grabbed a nearby chair and invited me to sit down with him in front of his locker. Here is what he said:

"I feel I have been terribly misunderstood. I think many Latin ballplayers have been misunderstood. We are thought to be moody, very temperamental, and every time we voice an opinion or a feeling that does not go along with everybody else, that label of moody is thrown up at us. That is not fair.

"For me, though, it has been more than that. People — sports writers write it and then other people say it — criticize that I whine and complain about every little thing that bothers me, every little ache and pain. Let me say that I play baseball very hard ... as hard as anyone, harder than most. I give everything I've got — running after fly balls, making throws, hitting the baseball, and running the bases. Sometimes I crash into walls catching balls or trying to catch them. I have even had stitches as a result. To me, it is the only way to play; it is the only way to do anything. I do everything to the best of my ability. I don't loaf or take it easy, no matter what the score is, no matter where our team is in the standings.

"It is the only way I know. And it is a matter of pride. I don't ever want anyone to say that Roberto Clemente gave less than his best. But, really, that is what they are saying when they talk about me being a hypochondriac, making excuses for not playing.

"When I miss a game, it is because I am not physically able to give my best. If I try to play and cannot get to a fly ball, cannot run fast enough to a base, cannot swing the bat to hit the ball hard because something hurts, then that is not the true Roberto Clemente. To me, that would be hurting the team. And, also, I could get myself hurt worse and end up missing many more games. I think it is the smart thing to miss a game or a few and get better. Then the Pittsburgh Pirates will have the real Roberto Clemente back in the lineup. I think that is what the Pittsburgh Pirates and their fans would want.

"Listen, I do not like to miss baseball games. I love the game. I love to play it. I love showing that men from Puerto Rico can play baseball very, very well. Why would I want to miss a chance to do that? It's just that going out there and just halfway playing because my shoulder or my back hurts … that would not be the whole Roberto Clemente. It would bother me deep down not to be able to get to a ball or hit a ball because something was hurting and to play poorly because of that.

"Don't you think that makes sense?"

I told Clemente that I thought it made a lot of sense, and I told him I was sorry that other writers chose to make him look bad instead of simply explaining his injuries and leaving it at that. I said that there is no way one person can know how much another person is hurting.

"That is exactly right," he said, the corners of his mouth turning up in a smile of appreciation that I understood him. "That is what I have been telling the writers. They stand beside me and nod their heads, like they agree. Then they write in their newspapers that Roberto Clemente is a hypochondriac, that he looks for reasons to stay out of games. That makes me sad and it makes me angry. But what can I do?"

Clemente's frustrations were evident, and I felt for him, knowing that newspapers and their writers usually have the last word, literally, and that the average person tends to believe what he or she reads. Whether intentional or not, writers had painted a picture of Clemente which was not at all accurate. He was depicted as looking for excuses not to play when, in fact, he wanted to play as much as he could and the best that he could.

This was always one of my favorite interviews. I could tell that Roberto Clemente, one of my three favorite baseball players of all time, completely trusted me even though he had never met me before. He sensed that I was sensitive to his feelings and that I would record and report them accurately.

I never saw Clemente again, not in person, anyway. He returned to the lineup a week later, getting a double and a home run and driving in two runs as the Pirates lost to the Mets. He finished the season with a .352 batting average.

As daylight brought a brand new year on January 1, 1973, I awoke from what I thought was a terrible dream. It was of Roberto Clemente dying in a plane crash. I was single in those days and always kept the radio on all night. That way, I would go to sleep listening to music and hear it when I woke up. I was half asleep when the newscaster announced that Clemente had been killed when an airplane went down in the Atlantic Ocean. It had been carrying supplies to earthquake-stricken Nicaragua, and Clemente was on board to make sure the food and other materials reached deserving victims.

When I shook off the cobwebs of sleep and realized my nightmare was reality, hearing the report of the tragedy once again, I was stunned. I recalled Clemente's many exciting feats on a baseball field and his many humanitarian efforts off it. I also recalled my treasured conversation with him, and I treasured it even more.

It was with great joy that I read in August of 1973 that the Baseball Writers Association of America had held a special election and waived the mandatory five-year waiting period for Clemente, voting him into the Hall of Fame. He compiled a .317 lifetime batting average with 240 home runs, 1,305 RBI, and four batting titles. Clemente became the first Hispanic player inducted at Cooperstown.

I never cared much for Bowie Kuhn as the Commissioner of major league baseball. But I thought what he said in his eulogy for Clemente was more appropriate than anything I read or heard: "He gave the term 'complete' a new meaning. He made the word superstar seem inadequate. He had about him a touch of royalty."

Chapter 17
Seeing Aaron Break the Record

A work assignment that is a fan's dream

As the 1974 baseball season began, the main topic of conversation was Hank Aaron breaking Babe Ruth's career home run record. It had stood since 1935 when the Babe retired with 714 homers. Aaron entered the '74 season one short of Ruth's record, and he tied it in the April 4 opener in Cincinnati.

The next day, Aaron was kept out of the lineup by the Atlanta Braves, who wanted their star to set the record at home. But Major League Baseball Commissioner Bowie Kuhn telephoned Braves manager Eddie Mathews and ordered him to start Aaron in the final game of the series in Cincinnati or face serious penalties. Aaron went 0-for-3, striking out twice and grounding out.

There was quite a bit of hubbub as everyone felt Kuhn had overstepped his authority by telling a manager he had to put a certain player in his lineup. Certainly it was not the first time a major league team had tried to arrange for a milestone to be reached in a player's home park. Kuhn was never a popular commissioner, and his dictatorial handling of this situation did nothing to improve his image in the baseball world.

I was working with *The Fayetteville Observer*, and while spring training was going on, I had met with the sports editor. I asked if Aaron had not broken Ruth's record by the time the Braves played their first home series, could I go down to Atlanta in hopes of covering a historic event. I was granted permission, but I would only be allowed to cover the first two games of the Braves' four-game series with the Los Angeles Dodgers. If it didn't happen by then, I would have to come home.

And so it was that I was among hundreds of newspaper, television, and radio reporters on hand for the Braves' home opener on Monday night, April 8, in Atlanta Fulton County Stadium. There were so many of us that an auxiliary press area was set up in the lower stands behind the Braves' dugout on the first-base side of the field. The attendance was listed at 53,775.

The Dodgers' starting pitcher was thirty-two-year-old Al Downing, a left-hander, who had come up with the New York Yankees and spent seven full seasons with them. Three years earlier, he had been a 20-game winner for the Dodgers. He set the Braves down in order in the first inning on three groundouts. Aaron, batting cleanup, walked to start the second and scored on Dusty Baker's double.

Darrell Evans led off the Braves' fourth, reaching on an error by Los Angeles shortstop Bill Russell. Downing threw a first-pitch fastball to Aaron, and he smashed it deep to left-center field. At the crack of the bat, people started rising, hoping and feeling the blast had enough to leave the park. It did. The ball soared over the fence and into the Braves' bullpen where lefty reliever Tom House caught it.

I jumped to my feet with everyone else, and we applauded as Aaron trotted around the bases like he always did, elbows held back and head held up, showing little emotion. Two teen-aged boys joined Aaron as he rounded second base, and he kept looking ahead as he continued his journey. I remember wondering, after all of the threats he had received, whether the sound and arrival of non-players wasn't a bit frightening. Aaron's mother awaited him at home plate, and she gave him a big hug. Atlanta players ran from the dugout to greet him, and the bullpen emptied as well, everybody sprinting out there to be part of the swarm at home plate. The ovation grew louder and went on for several minutes.

Aaron batted twice more in the game, grounding out both times. It must have been hard to concentrate for those at-bats. The Braves won, 7-4, despite getting only four hits as they took advantage of six Los Angeles errors to score four unearned runs.

After the game, the Atlanta locker room was packed as reporters jammed around Aaron to record his comments. Microphones were shoved toward his face, and all of us writers tried desperately to make enough room to be able to scribble quotes onto our note pads.

"Tonight changes a lot of things," Aaron said during his remarks to the media throng. "To break a record held by Mr. Ruth for thirty-nine years has given me some of the recognition I've been slighted while working hard for years. I'd now like to go on to break Stan Musial's league record for most hits."

Aaron did that, finishing his career with 3,771 hits, third on the all-time list behind Pete Rose (4,256) and Ty Cobb (4,189). Aaron's 755 home runs are second behind Barry Bonds' controversial total of 762.

The hate letters that flooded the Atlanta Braves' mailbox took a toll on Aaron. After ending the 1973 season with 713 home runs, Aaron spent a nerve-racking winter that brought an onslaught of death threats and letters dripping with ugliness.

A sample follows: "Dear Nigger Henry, It has come to my attention that you are going to break Babe Ruth's record. I don't think you are going to break this record established by the great Babe Ruth if I can help it. I don't think that any coon should ever play baseball. Whites are far more superior than jungle bunnies. I will be going to the rest of your games and if you hit one more home run it will be your last.

My gun is watching your every black move. This is no joke."

Thousands of letters were sent from all over the country. Some people even suggested that Aaron stop trying to hit home runs; in fact, many letters advised him to simply retire from baseball and, thus, leave the record intact. It was estimated that Aaron received about 3,000 letters per day. A large number of them were filled with racism and hatred.

The general public assumed the mail was coming from a bunch of nuts and that the threats were empty. Discounting such threats was quite another matter for the man to whom the hatred was directed. Hank Aaron was on the receiving end because of the color of his skin and because he was talented enough to be on the brink of breaking baseball's most glamorous record, one set by the game's most enamored star of all time.

I was fortunate in that, unlike most of the writers and broadcasters in the Braves' locker room, I was not up against a pressing deadline. *The Fayetteville Observer* at that time was an afternoon newspaper, meaning my deadline was not until the next day. I had all night to write my game story and column. As a result, I hung around a long time after the press conference, patiently awaiting an opportunity to have Aaron all to myself for a few minutes.

He was kind enough to grant me a private audience, and he answered my questions while standing in front of his locker and peeling off his uniform.

Knowing that Aaron had endured threats of death and harm to his family, along with other ugly, insulting letters — almost all centered on race and animosity of racists upset over the idea of a black man breaking a white man's record — I asked him if hitting No. 715 was more of a joy or a relief.

Aaron smiled and shook his head. "It should be all joy, shouldn't it? And, probably on down the road, I will feel a lot more joy. But, right now, to be honest with you, it's relief ... a big load off my shoulders. As you get close to a record, the pressure builds up because everyone is asking, talking, and writing about it. You tell yourself it's just another home run, but it's not.

"The bad part, though, what really made it tense, was the letters and phone calls with the threats and racial insults. You think the people making those threats are just a bunch of nuts and nothing will come of it, but you never know. People do a lot of awful things. Yes, I have been worried. You would be, too."

I asked if Aaron thought breaking Ruth's record had earned him respect that he felt had not been given him.

"Respect, that's a good word, and I guess that's what I have wanted. You know, I have worked hard to be the best baseball player I could be. Everybody talks about me being a natural hitter; they make it sound like all I have to do is whip my wrists, and the ball goes flying over the fence.

"God has given me some gifts. I know that, and I appreciate that. But I have still had to work, and I have worked hard. I have read and heard many times that I make this game look easy, and I think because of that, people don't think I'm trying hard. I always try hard. I always work my hardest and try my hardest. I want people to realize that."

Wrinkling his brow, Aaron said, "It's kind of sad, isn't it, that it took breaking Mr. Ruth's home run record for people to realize I'm a pretty good ball player? I know there are a lot of very good ones — past and present — and I'm not saying I'm the best. I'm just saying I think I'm among them, and I would like to be given that respect you mentioned."

I remember thinking that is was very strange that Kuhn did not attend the game. He sent a message that he had another commitment and dispensed Monte Irvin, who worked in the commissioner's office, to represent him. When Irvin, a Hall of Fame outfielder, walked onto the field, the Fulton County Stadium crowd booed. The boos were obviously intended for Kuhn. The fans did not understand why the commissioner wasn't there, and I couldn't either. It was an obvious slight to Aaron. What could have been more important than being there to shake the hand of the man who broke baseball's most hallowed record? Kuhn's failure to attend Aaron's record-setting feat was, to me, the distinguishing mark of his tenure as commissioner. And a sorry tenure it was, in my opinion.

I ended up staying in the clubhouse for a long time, not leaving until several hours after the game was over. I was one of the last few people to leave, walking out the door along with Braves catcher Johnny Oates. He had driven in what proved to be the decisive run for Atlanta, snapping a 4-4 tie with an RBI fielder's choice while pinch hitting for winning pitcher Ron Reed.

Johnny and I had been fourth-grade classmates at Seventy-First School in Fayetteville, and we did a lot of catching up. I asked him about his college days at Virginia Tech and about his life as a major league player. I was happy for Oates and took pride in the fact that he became an outstanding big league manager years later.

Since my paper had given permission for me to stay for two games, I remained in Atlanta for the next night's contest. Fewer than 11,000 fans showed up. Right-hander Don Sutton, who is with Aaron in the Base-ball Hall of Fame, pitched seven innings of five-hit ball as the Dodgers beat the Braves, 9-2. Aaron did not play. It was career victory No. 122 for Sutton, who would go on to win 324 games in the majors.

A footnote to the game is that long before it started, I had a short visit with Sutton as he sat in the trainer's room. There was no inter-view as that was prohibited since he was the starting pitcher. I was allowed to hand him a note which was sent from one of my best friends, Ron Sellers. Ron had been Sutton's lieutenant while both were serving in the Army, and they had become friends. When I told Sutton why I was there, he shared with me how much he thought of Ron and told me a few things to relay back to him.

Sutton mentioned that, while he was not glad Downing would be the pitcher forever linked to Aaron's history-making blast, he was happy it wasn't him instead. "I had that on my mind when we came down here," Sutton said, "and I'm relieved I wasn't the one to give up number 715. But Aaron has hit three homers off of me, and no matter what, I still contributed my share to the total."

I found the long list of all the pitchers victimized by Aaron. Some of the names included Whammy Douglas, Corky Valentine, and Art Caccerelli. There was a Rabe and a Mabe, a Nye and a Hook, an R. Miller and an R.L. Miller, a Veale and a Lamb, three different Jack-sons, a Morehead and Moorhead, and a Brewer, Boozer, and Barr.

Like most fans, I have my opinions about Bonds and steroids. Much of what I have read, not to mention his physical appear-ance, makes me believe he was a user. And that makes me view his records as tainted. I still consider Hank Aaron to be baseball's home run king.

Chapter 18
My Baseball Comeback

A surprising return to active duty on the baseball diamond

There was never a question of whether I would attend college. My parents had always stressed education and the importance of continuing it after high school. I was happy about that; I wanted to go to college. At the same time, I never had any career goals or definite plans for what I would study when I got there. Medicine was out because I did not have the slightest aptitude for science. Working in business didn't interest me, and neither did being a lawyer.

I was not prepared for college. That was no fault of my high school teachers or my high school in general. It was me. I was a lazy student, one who made good grades mostly by memorizing. I could always do that. Give me a list of definitions, French vocabulary words, or dates in history, and I could spit them onto a test paper with near perfection. The trouble was that I did not actually learn a lot, and memorized facts are usually forgotten quickly.

I will say that I learned a great deal of English. I completely understood all of the punctuation rules and which parts of speech did what. Conjugating verbs was a snap for me, and I never had a problem with using the wrong tense or making nouns and verbs agree. Math was an entirely different matter. I could figure batting averages in my head in a few seconds, and freshman algebra made good sense, but I got tangled in the triangles of tenth-grade geometry and struggled through advanced math courses my last two years of high school. I was afraid math would be my undoing in college.

Ten boys from our senior class were heading to the University of North Carolina at Chapel Hill, and most of them couldn't wait for a life of freedom and partying. I did not feel at all prepared for college and was afraid I would flunk out. I have never been a party person because I have never been a drinker. I enjoyed life as it was and did not feel the need to find something to help me have a good time. I tasted beer and gagged. I had expected it to taste like ginger ale; instead, it tasted like I thought urine would taste. My fear of college was extreme. I wouldn't even buy a UNC sticker to put on our family car's rear window like everybody else was doing. I did not want people pointing at our car and laughing when I flunked out of school. Although I desperately wanted a college diploma, I was never confident of attaining one.

The Vietnam War was going on, and during my freshman year in college, student draft deferments depended on being in a certain percentile of one's class, based on grade-point average. I knew I was safe for the first semester, but if I didn't make at least a 2.0 GPA, my draft status could change. That provided extra incentive, although I already had plenty. Boosted by an A in trigonometry, I cleared the 2.0 hurdle with plenty to spare, and my confidence received a substantial jolt because of my math grade.

Sometime during the second semester of my freshman year, I received a letter in the mail from the Selective Service. It said my draft status had been changed to 1-A. I was petrified. I knew my grades were good, that the 1-A was a mistake. I also knew mistakes had been drafted into the Army, and I wanted to make sure that didn't happen to me. I wasted no time. That very day, I walked out to the main highway, stuck my thumb out, and I hitched a ride to Fayetteville.

I walked into the Selective Service office, and I stated my case, explaining that I should not be classified 1-A. The lady excused herself, made a phone call, came back, and apologized, agreeing the letter I had received was an error. She said I would receive a correction and a return to my deferred status within a few days. I phoned home, and my daddy picked me up a short while later. Over a home-cooked meal which tasted especially delicious after the successful trip to the draft office, I told my parents about my adventure. Daddy drove me back to Chapel Hill that night.

It was February, in the middle of the second semester of my junior year at Carolina when I found out I was headed in the wrong direction career-wise. I was majoring in journalism, with an emphasis in advertising. I chose advertising because I thought I could earn quite a bit of money. However, I fared terribly in the courses. One day, after class, the man who taught the advertising courses asked me to wait a minute so he could talk with me. He had enjoyed twenty-five successful years on Madison Avenue, writing copy for some of the most renowned advertising firms in America. He knew what he was talking about, and he told me that I did not have what it took in that profession.

To tell the truth, I was not all that enthused about advertising, so I guess what he said made it easy to move on. That same day, I decided upon something that really excited me. I was already in the journalism department, I felt I was a halfway decent writer, and I had always loved sports. So I decided to be a sports writer. It was not a decision I pored over, but it was one I felt very good about. When I called my mother and told her, she felt good about it, too.

The most helpful and important course in my major was Community Journalism, which I took during my senior year. There was no text book and there were no classes. The professor required students to find part-time newspaper jobs for no pay, write stories for the paper, and slip clippings of the stories under his door. I worked with the sports department of my local newspaper, covering high school football and basketball games on weekends. The sports editor, a brusque, set-in-his-ways bachelor named Ed Seaman, taught me more than any college professor had.

There were no computers used as word processors in news rooms back then, and we used old Royal typewriters to tap out our stories on sheets of copy paper. My first few stories were filled with red after Mr. Seaman deleted and simplified much of what I had written. The sea of red dried up as the weeks passed, and I wrote crisper, more concise pieces. I earned an A in the course and received a job offer in the process.

My starting salary was $105 a week, $5,460 per year. I thought I was in high cotton. Earning a weekly paycheck of $100 qualified as the big time as far as I was concerned. I bought a used car, a 1967 white Camaro, giving me monthly car and insurance payments. I lived with my family for a while, and I saved up the money to pay cash for a clothes washer and dryer. When I purchased them, I moved out and rented a small apartment.

I did not work in sports at first. I covered district court, wrote obituaries, and handled re-writes of press releases. It wasn't exciting, but I loved the newsroom atmosphere, and I was learning newspaper writing and editing style. My first summer was more of an education than all four years of college stacked together.

I listened as people blatantly lied under oath. I witnessed some of the most entertaining theatrics, and they were staged in courtrooms by lawyers. I attended a trial in which a judge sentenced a long-haired young man to six months in jail, with the sentence to be suspended if the defendant returned after the lunch break with a "regular" haircut, which he did. I saw people who were obviously guilty walk into the sunshine and fresh air because they had money and connections. The old courthouse was quite a school.

After six months of working on the news side, there was an opening in sports. Mr. Seaman had told me he would bring me onto his staff when the opportunity arose, and he did. I changed desks and responsibilities in early December, when college basketball was getting into full swing. The timing could not have been better.

Being a sports writer was the ideal job for me. I could not believe that I could earn a living by attending sports events. I thought life could not get any better than watching Atlantic Coast Conference basketball games and getting paid for it. I worked some weird hours and many, many weekends, but I didn't care. There was a certain rush from sitting in a crowded newsroom, anxiously writing to meet deadlines while knowing everybody around me was doing the same thing.

It was a thrill to witness the sensational exploits of Michael Jordan, David Thompson, and so many other terrific college basketball players. I was also able to cover one of the most monumental feats in baseball history as I was on hand for the game in which Hank Aaron hit his 715th home run, breaking Babe Ruth's record.

Over the years, I was fortunate to conduct one-on-one interviews with such sports figures as Jordan, Thompson, Jack Nicklaus, Dean Smith, Roberto Clemente, Willie Stargell, Billy Cunningham, Pete Rose, John Wooden, Nancy Lopez, Chris Evert, Kay Yow, Phil Niekro, and Dale Murphy, among others. I became a decent writer and an even better interviewer, asking questions and conversing with these men and women in a way that made them feel comfortable enough to share some deep emotions.

While at the University of North Carolina, I tore up my left knee playing freshman baseball in the fall of my first year. I was playing left field, and I jumped to make a catch against the fence. My foot caught in the wire, and something in my knee crunched as I jumped. It crunched again when I was coming down. I ripped ligaments and cartilage in the knee, but did not have surgery for more than two years. During that period, I was on and off crutches, hobbling badly when I happened to twist the knee or when it occasionally caught as I was climbing steps.

My knee was operated on during spring break of my junior year at Carolina. Doctors were not performing arthroscopic surgery at the time, and there was a long zipper where the surgeon had gone in to repair ligaments and remove cartilage. Because so much tissue had been sliced through, recovery took quite a while. I walked with crutches for six weeks, and I was bothered by considerable soreness and stiffness even after that. That was 1967, and by the time my knee felt fairly normal again, it was time to begin my senior year.

It was the summer of 1968 when I was able to play baseball again — for the first time since the fall of 1964, a stretch of three and a half years. I rejoined the Fayetteville Cardinals, but I was an entirely different player. Although my knee had completely healed, it was always a bit stiff, and I never regained full flexibility. I was not in pain, but my knee felt sore whenever I ran for very long, and the little bit of speed I once possessed was gone.

My inability to run or move well limited me to playing first base and third base, and I put in occasional corner outfield duty when there was no one else to play out there. I batted over .300 each of my three additional seasons with the Cardinals, with a high of .353, but I hit a total of just four home runs. My left knee, the one I had injured, was the pivotal one since I batted left-handed. Because of the lack of flexibility in that knee, I could not turn it the way I needed to in order to open my hips and produce the bat speed required to generate power. Every once in a while, I would take a low, inside pitch and deposit it over the short fence down the right-field line in Jim Hodges Park, but for the most part, I hit the ball up the middle and from one gap to the other. But I was playing baseball again. And that was a great feeling.

I met my wife while covering a basketball game at what was then known as Pembroke State University (now UNC Pembroke). She was sitting in the stands across the court from the press table. Although she was right in the middle of a throng of students packed together like sardines, she was so beautiful that she seemed to almost jump out from the others sitting in the bleachers.

My sister, Judy, was also a student at Pembroke, and she was at the game. I met her in the concession area at halftime, and I was describing to her the dazzling young lady I had seen. I was hoping Judy would know her and could introduce me to her. About that time, she walked by, and my sister said that, yes, she knew her. She said her name was Dahlia Wade and that, yes, she would ask if she would like to be introduced to me after the game.

Dahlia and I have been married nearly 35 years now. We had a grand chance to get to know each other before having children, the first coming after six and a half years of marriage. My wife and I attended Lamaze classes before both girls were born. The teacher listed several aids husbands could utilize to help their wives during labor. Among them were a wash cloth dampened with cool water, for sucking moisture or applying to hot areas like the forehead and neck, and a rubber ball, to be rolled over the small of the back.

The only trouble was that Dahlia wanted all three things done at the same time, and I only had two hands. Whichever of those things I was doing, Dahlia requested — no, demanded — one of the other two. When the pain became the most intense, just before Erika was born, my wife screamed, "We're getting separate bedrooms, because I'm never going to let this happen again." Fortunately, we continued sharing the same bedroom, and Laura was born five and a half years later.

Our daughters are both very beautiful and very bright, traits handed down directly from their mother. Erika graduated from Duke University and Laura from Boston College, both walking across the stage after what seemed like just a few weeks of childhood. At least, that's the way it seemed to me. Being a dad has been the most fabulous, adventuresome experience. Both girls played sports, excelled academically in high school and college, and they have always treated people with respect and kindness.

Slow-pitch softball entered my life in a humorously ironic way. When I was in college, working my summer jobs as a daytime baseball instructor and evening umpire, I saw my first slow-pitch game. The baseball games I was assigned to umpire were called off one night, and I was asked to keep the official scorebook for a softball game.

The city fire department and the police department were matched up, and my impression was that the contest was nothing more than a bunch of old men moving around in extremely slow motion. I thought the high, lazy arc of the pitches was laughable, and shaking my head, I said to myself that this was one game I would never play.

Five years later, discovering there was no longer a baseball team I could play with, I helped my church organize a softball team. Slow-pitch was the closest thing to baseball that I could play, and I tore into it. I played hard, pushing teammates to do the same, and I played to win. Sometimes, I overdid it, and I learned to back off a little. In a few years, we were one of the better church league teams in the city.

The game I had once made fun of had become a game I loved. Those "old men" I had watched trying to hit the big ball with the big arc now included me. I was still in my twenties, but the point is that what I thought was an old man's game took on a different perspective when I was one of the players. I played slow-pitch softball with a passion, diving for ground balls from my shortstop position, hustling to take an extra base, and never hesitating to slide into second, third, or home when there was a chance the play would be close. I played the game just as I had played baseball — as hard as I could.

Ron Sellers, a close friend since childhood, was one of my church league teammates. He had been an outstanding high school pitcher, and he still possessed a live arm and a wide assortment of breaking pitches. On weekends, he was pitching for the Rex Raiders, a semi-pro team from a neighboring county. One day, Ron asked me if I would like to pitch for the Raiders. He explained that they had a doubleheader coming up the following weekend, on Mother's Day. He was going to pitch one game, and the other two regular pitchers were going to be out of town, so an emergency starter was needed.

I laughed, saying I had never pitched, other than batting practice. But I agreed to give it a try, and I met Ron at a local baseball diamond and threw twenty or thirty balls to him from the mound. Most of them were in or near the strike zone, and I was even able to break off a respectable curveball or two. I was two months short of my thirty-fourth birthday and was as excited as a kid over my pitching debut.

All day Saturday, I practiced different windups. I decided to go with an abbreviated version, really a no-windup delivery. I figured throwing my arms around would only detract from my concentration and my control. Besides, I might burn extra energy with an elaborate windup, and I needed all the energy I could muster. One thing I knew was that the legs are as important as the arm to a pitcher. I also knew I didn't possess a lot of speed and that I would need to push off the rubber with my right leg in order to generate enough speed to have some semblance of a fastball.

The (no)windup I settled on involved bringing my hands to my belt, swiveling my body to the right, pushing off the rubber, pulling my right arm behind me, leading with my left shoulder, and letting the ball fly. Using this type of delivery provided one additional advantage in that very little modification would be needed when runners reached base and I had to go into my stretch. About the only difference was that I would begin with the right side of my right foot against the rubber and my body already turned so that I was facing third base instead of looking head-on toward the plate.

I kept doing phantom windups — with no ball or glove — so much that, without thinking, I did a couple when Dahlia and I were in the grocery store. When my wife glared at me, I said, "What?" And she told me to quit acting like the "other" kids, who pretended to play baseball wherever they were.

That night, after the lights were out and we were in bed, I lay there staring toward the ceiling into the blackness. I was too excited to sleep … and a little concerned that I might embarrass myself the next day. Suddenly, it hit me that I had not decided on how I would grip the ball for different pitches. I slipped out of bed and moved as quietly as I could so I wouldn't wake my wife. I went to one of our spare bedrooms, opened a bureau drawer where I kept a baseball, and I took it out. I sat on the couch in our den. I turned on a lamp in order to see the threads on the ball. I experimented, holding my fingers with the seams, across them, and between them. I remembered what I had been told about movement achieved with a variety of grips.

Then I decided that I should practice gripping the ball for different pitches while it was in my glove. I needed to be able to do that without tipping my pitches — alerting the other team which pitch I was throwing before I threw it. I crept to the spare bedroom closet, where we hung coats, stored the vacuum cleaner, leaned umbrellas against the wall, and stacked blankets on the top shelf. I kept my glove, a Wilson Ted Sizemore model, under an old quilt. I pulled it down and padded barefoot to the foyer, where a large mirror hung. I put the glove on my left hand, held the ball in my right, and watched myself in the mirror as I pretended to pitch.

I did several repetitions with my no-windup windup and my

stretch position, trying both while taking grips on the ball required for throwing two kinds of fastballs (with and across the seams) and my curveball. After about a half an hour, satisfied that I could grip the seams smoothly and without looking at the ball to do it, I put my glove on the stool in the kitchen, ready to be grabbed as I headed out the door the next day. I placed the ball back into the drawer, and I went back to bed. I still did not feel sleepy, but sometime between three in the morning and daybreak, I dozed off and slept soundly.

That Sunday, after attending church with my wife and taking my mother out to lunch, I went home and changed into Bermuda shorts and a golf shirt. My wife, not nearly as excited about my baseball comeback as I was, said she thought she would stay home and take a nap. She wished me luck and said she looked forward to my telling her all about my adventure when I got home. I drove to my parents' house, picked up with my daddy, and we set out for Lillington, which would be the home team and the Rex Raiders' opponent for the doubleheader. The distance to Lillington was about twenty miles, and it took us twenty-eight minutes. Lillington was a tiny town (today, it is small) with a few stores and a blinking light to warn of an upcoming railroad track. About a half mile past the "business district" stood several pine trees, and on one of them, a piece of a cardboard box was tacked. On the brown surface, the words Game Today had been scrawled in black crayon with an arrow pointing to the right.

I made a right turn onto a dirt road and followed it through a tobacco field which wound on and on before becoming a field of tall, green grass that would be harvested as golden hay. Smack dab in the middle of the hayfield was the ball field.

Uneven bleachers consisted of long slats of boards, which were gray and warped, weather beaten by years of rain and sunshine. The boards sat precariously on support structures made of iron. In some places the boards were attached to the support structures, but just as many were unattached and wobbled when someone stepped on them. Pieces of tin covered the seats, giving the impression of grandstands. Fifteen or so feet in front of the bleachers was a backstop constructed of chicken wire that was rusted and dotted with numerous holes eaten into the tiny octagons by time. The holes were not repaired; instead, they were closed together with what amounted to wire twist ties. The dugouts resembled coffins in appearance and size, wooden rectangles lying on their sides and open for viewing. The seating capacity in those little boxes looked to be fourteen or fifteen if occupants were packed like sardines in a can. Beside the visitors' dugout, which was located down the third-base line, was a small American flag on a short wooden pole stuck into a holder like the ones seen in VFW halls. Next to the home dugout was a much larger confederate flag.

What passed as a grass infield had more bare spots than actual grass, and patches of weeds threatened to take over the cutouts in front of each base. The outfield grass needed mowing, and there were three circles of dirt where outfielders had habitually positioned themselves. The most attractive feature of the Lillington ball park was its outfield fence. A row of freshly painted white pickets stretched in a semi-circle from one foul line to the other, with distances from home plate marked with black numbers. They said 310 in right field, 372 in center, and 307 in left. I thought the small dimensions might have something to do with snatching as little farm land as possible for the ball park.

When I opened the car door to get out, I noted that it was eleven minutes after two. Ron had told me the first game was scheduled to start at 1:30 and that I should get there by 2:30. That would give me plenty of time to receive a uniform and change into it.

The day was a scorcher — 97 degrees with 95 percent humidity. The sun was beating down on the field like a spotlight. People in attendance wore shorts, T-shirts, tank tops, assorted ball caps, and straw hats. More of them sat in lawn chairs on either side of and in front of the bleachers than on the unsteady boards. Safety was probably as much of a factor as comfort in the matter of seating choice.

I walked over to the Raiders' dugout and waited outside. Ron was pitching the first game of the doubleheader, and he was trailing, 1-0, in the sixth inning. When he retired the side, he came over to where I was standing and invited me into the dugout. He quickly introduced me around, and I was handed a uniform and a hat by one of the players. I went back to my car to change clothes, and I was pleased that the pants and shirt fit fairly well. The uniform was not particularly attractive, though it was eye-catching. It was dark gold trimmed with brown, and the cap was brown with an R on the front. The stockings were also brown. I was happy just to be wearing a baseball uniform again.

Beneath the uniform, I wore a baseball undershirt, commonly known as sleeves. I did not have brown, so I had brought navy blue. The sleeves were long; I had worn long ones since my Little League days. It seemed a strange habit in oppressive temperatures, but the sleeves absorbed perspiration and kept it from rolling onto my hands. And I sweated a lot.

The Raiders' manager, who was to be my catcher, was a tall man with skin the color of milk chocolate and a voice just as rich and pleasant. His name was Robert Ray, and his countenance suggested confidence and leadership. He had muscular arms and shoulders so wide they made his chest protector look kiddy-sized. Robert put his arm around me and said we would keep our signals simple. A fist would be for a fastball, one finger would be for a curve, and so on. He asked how many pitches I had, and I said just the two he had mentioned.

Robert handed me a baseball and walked away from me, pacing off the distance between a pitcher's rubber and home plate. He had done that so many times that 60 feet and six inches were practically programmed into his step. When he finished pacing, Robert turned around, dropped his cap on the ground for a plate, and crouched in a catcher's stance. He held up his big mitt and said, "Let's see what you've got."

The ball felt so light in my right hand, so good the way it fit in my palm. Holding a baseball and preparing to throw it made me tingle inside. After ten or twelve pitches, the big catcher walked a few feet in front of his hat and said, "Go ahead and cut loose with your fastball …" and "… I thought you said you only had two pitches. But that's a pretty good sinker you've got there."

I almost laughed and answered, "First of all, I am cutting loose, and second, the ball is sinking from lack of speed."

I was excited as game time approached, and I was noticeably nervous. I felt pretty sure I could get the ball across the plate, but I was unsure what the batters would do with my pitches. I envisioned them hitting more than a few over the short picket fence.

The first game had ended, 1-0, with Ron pitching a four-hitter and striking out eleven. Behind him, the Raiders managed just two singles and committed three errors, one leading to an unearned run. Always an optimist, Ron patted me on the back and said, "The boys have saved the runs for you. You're going to win this one."

The Raiders made Ron a profit right away, bunching together four base hits and scoring two runs in the top of the first inning. My legs were shaky as I took the mound, my first warm-up toss sailing all the way to the backstop and my second bouncing ten feet in front of the plate. Everything smoothed out after that, and my last few warm-ups were good ones.

My first pitch of the game was right down the middle. The leadoff batter took it, then popped up the second pitch to our shortstop. I fell behind the second hitter, two balls and no strikes, and he tattooed the next pitch. Luckily, he got under it a little, and our center fielder made the catch a couple of feet from the fence. The number three hitter tapped a first-pitch one-hopper right back to me, and I trotted off the field following a six-pitch inning.

Sitting in the dugout, I found that I was breathing hard and that I could feel my heart almost jumping out of my chest. It was adrenalin. I took a bunch of deep breaths, exhaling slowly, and I sipped a little paper cup of water. I was so thirsty that I wanted to gulp down one cup of water after another, but I knew doing that would make me nauseous. When it was time to return to the mound, I walked slowly, trying to calm myself down and avoid rapidly burning every ounce of energy I had.

I gave up a one-out double in the second inning and left the runner stranded by getting my first strikeout and a grounder to short. I was experimenting as I went along, trying different grips on my so-called fastball. Occasionally, I threw it side-armed, putting my first two fingers between the seams of the ball. That delivery was particularly effective on right-handed batters as the ball ran in on them. A couple of the Lillington hitters bailed out when I went side-arm. My natural motion was overhand, straight over the top, and I found that the most effective way to throw that fastball was with my fingers parallel with the seams. I got more sinking movement that way, and increasing pressure with my middle finger created movement that was down and away from left-handed batters and jammed the right-handed hitters. That was the pitch I used most. My curveball became better as I went along, as I learned to snap it off more and get a tighter spin as a result. I started to feel like a pitcher out there.

Back on the bench, I felt more relaxed, and when I looked at my chest, the letter D in RAIDERS was not doing the rumba any more. I took a sip of water, rinsed my cottony mouth, and spit it out. Then I swallowed a little. I drew myself a second cup of water from the yellow five-gallon plastic container, removed my cap, and poured that one over my head. Boy, did that feel good.

Two Lillington batters reached in the third, one on my first walk, but I escaped without giving up a run when a hard-hit line drive was caught by our first baseman, who stepped on the bag for a double play.

I never liked the designated hitter rule, but I was grateful that it was used in the Rex Raiders' league. I could not imagine standing in the batter's box and facing fastballs thrown by youngsters with strong, live arms. The opposing pitcher threw very hard — after seeing nothing but lazily tossed softballs for so long, his speedballs seemed like bullets — and I was glad I didn't have to walk up to the plate with a bat in my hands.

The fourth ended when Lillington lined back-to-back two-out hits, only to run itself out of the inning. The first of the two batters went from first to third on the second single, and when our second baseman bobbled the throw back to the infield, he broke for home. Seeing that the ball was recovered quickly, he tried to return to third and was trapped. In the ensuing rundown, I covered home and tagged the runner for the last out.

As I sat and cheered for my teammates to score some more runs, I thought about how great it felt to be playing baseball again. It didn't matter that it was in the middle of a hay field or that the bleachers and dugout might blow over if a light breeze came up. I didn't care that our uniforms were trimmed in brown. It would have been fine if no one was there to watch the game. The main thing was that I was playing … playing baseball, The Game. I felt a silly grin spreading across my face and knew I must have looked like a little boy who just found out that he could be granted a wish. And I guess that's what I was — a boy again. I sat there, thinking how fortunate I was to have another chance to wear a baseball uniform and participate in a baseball game. It was super stuff. Meanwhile, the Raiders cashed in on two walks and an error, tacking on a single and a double to add three runs for a 5-0 lead.

In the bottom of the fifth, I walked the leadoff batter and paid for it when he scored on a two-out double. Over the five innings, I notched four strikeouts, all swinging, when the batters were far out in front of my fastballs. They did not adjust to how slowly I was throwing the ball.

While our team batted, I leaned back and tried to rest. I was still mentally enjoying the moment, glad to be there and to be pitching, but my body did not seem to be cooperating with my mind. I closed my eyes and envisioned a runner who was leading the pack with a few yards to go before he reached the finish line, and his legs froze. He could not move another step. I opened my eyes, tapped my feet on the dirt to make sure they could move, and I forced my psyche to out-bid my physique. Kind of like the angel on one shoulder making the devil on the other shoulder go poof.

The leadoff man in the sixth lined a single right past my head. I went into my stretch and checked the runner. He had taken such a huge lead off first — it must have been twenty feet — that I was shocked. Either he was going to steal and didn't figure I would no-tice, or he didn't get on base much and wasn't sure what to do when he did. I stepped back off the rubber and threw to my first baseman, easily picking off the runner. It was a gift out, a gimme.

It was a good thing, too, because the next batter jumped on my first pitch and clouted it deep to left field. I didn't even need to turn around to know it was a home run, but I did watch admiringly to see where the ball would land. I'm not sure it did. It might have gone into orbit. That narrowed our lead to 5-2.

Not knowing what happened, I was amazed at how strong I felt when I returned to the dugout. I suddenly believed I could go the dis-tance, throw a complete game. It was a gigantic second wind. I said a silent prayer of gratitude and geared up to pitch three more innings.

I retired Lillington in order in the seventh, but the home-team hitters were starting to time my pitches, and all three outs were on hard-hit balls. One was a smash back through the box. I threw my glove up, more as a reflex than anything else, knocked the ball down and lobbed it to first.

Between innings, I noticed I was growing tired, really tired. All of the adrenalin had been used up. So had most of my energy. My legs felt heavy. My right arm seemed a little dead. My under sleeves were soaked, and my uniform jersey was completely wet as well. Sweat dripped off the bill of my cap. I didn't know how much longer I could last.

I got an out in the eighth on a scorching grounder that our short-stop made a fine play on, and then I walked the next batter on four pitches. None of them was even close. Robert called time out, took off his mask, and walked slowly to the mound. I knew why. My legs were rubbery, and when I breathed deeply, trying to reach down for something extra, the tank was empty. I was wondering if I could stand up, much less throw another pitch.

"Man, you gave us a good game today," he said, "but I think you've had it. I don't think you have anything left." I agreed and accepted pats on the back from my infielders before trotting to the dugout. Our shortstop went to the mound and threw nothing but fastballs to get the last five outs of the game. The Lillington hitters were late on those fastballs after seeing such slow ones from me.

The Raiders scored another run and won, 6-2. I was the winning pitcher. I had allowed two runs, both earned, and seven hits, while striking out five and walking three in seven and one-third innings. I was very pleased, and I had a whole lot of fun.

So much fun that I thought I wanted to pitch again, and Ron as-sured me I would be welcome. But the thought of playing every Sun-day made me decide to quit while I was ahead and stick with softball.

I still think of my comeback sometimes, of that bright, sunny afternoon on the mound of a little ball field in a little town. I can remember almost every pitch I made.

Chapter 19
Taking Dad to Atlanta

Annual pilgrimages to watch the beloved Braves

Every boy who has been taken to a ball game by his dad remembers that grand experience. When the boy becomes a man, he has the chance to re-live those happy memories by reciprocating.

I was glad to have that opportunity. In fact, I took my daddy to several major league games in Atlanta. He still pulled for the Pirates, so the first few times we drove down for games, I made sure Pittsburgh would be the visiting team. On our first road trip to Atlanta, we left very early on Saturday morning, August 1, 1970, for the Braves' game with the Pirates that afternoon. Tickets were awaiting us at the will call window for that contest as well as for Sunday's series finale.

The Braves' media relations department had been kind enough to grant my request for a press pass and complimentary tickets for both games. I used the press pass to visit Pittsburgh's locker room prior to the game so I could talk with Roberto Clemente. Then I sat with Dad in the stands. We had excellent seats, located about twenty rows back from the field in between home plate and the third-base dugout, where the Pirates resided.

Both teams were loaded with offensive weapons. Pittsburgh was led by Willie Stargell, Roberto Clemente, Al Oliver, and Manny Sanguillen. Atlanta's big bats were Hank Aaron, Orlando Cepeda, Felix Millan, and Rico Carty. Stargell, Clemente, Aaron, and Cepeda would be elected to the Hall of Fame. Carty was on his way to winning the National League batting title.

My daddy and I were extremely disappointed that Clemente could not play. He had been out with an injury since July 25, but our hopes were boosted by his pinch-running appearance the night before. When the lineups were posted on the scoreboard, however, Clemente's name was not listed.

The first pitch was thrown at a made-for-TV game time of 3:10 in the afternoon, and it was blistering hot. Fortunately, we were sitting in an area that would be in the shade in a couple of innings when the sun moved behind the stadium on the first-base side. Atlanta starting pitcher George Stone, a left-hander, retired Pittsburgh leadoff batter Johnny Jeter on a ground ball to shortstop, and that was the only out he got. A triple, two singles, and a double were sandwiched around a hit batsman, sending Stone to the showers. By the time the smoke had cleared, the Pirates had scored five runs.

Aaron smacked a home run with a man on, and the Braves tacked on another run to cut their deficit to 5-3. We were not going to see a pitcher's duel, and that was fine with Dad and me. Watching bats boom and runners circle the bases was fun.

Stargell bashed a three-run homer, and Tony Gonzalez belted a two-run shot for Atlanta, highlighting a continuous attack by both teams, and after six innings, the Pirates led, 10-6. What followed was the most explosive inning I have ever witnessed.

Jeter tripled with one out to ignite Pittsburgh in the seventh, and Dave Cash walked. Oliver's double plated Jeter. Sanguillen drove in a pair with a single. First baseman Bob Robertson, a big, muscular guy, crushed a Julio Navarro pitch for his second home run in as many games, a two-run shot. Stargell came up next and blasted his second homer of the game, his twentieth of the season. Jose Pagan was the next hitter, and he also hit a home run. The Pirates scored seven times to take a 17-6 lead.

Dad and I were still shaking our heads, when Gonzalez singled in a run for the Braves and then came around on Aaron's second home run of the day. Before the fans could get back in their seats, Carty sent a towering drive into the seats. We were astonished. We had just seen back-to-back home runs after seeing back-to-back-to-back homers in the top of the inning. Five home runs in the same inning!

Pittsburgh won, 20-10. The Pirates pounded out 22 hits, 14 of them for extra bases, and the Braves had 15 hits. There were eight home runs. Robertson and Stargell each had five hits. Stargell doubled three times, giving him 14 total bases, and drove in six runs. Pagan had four hits and four RBI. Aaron's two home runs were his 29th and 30th. His five RBI brought his season's total to 90.

Dad and I were in no hurry to leave the ball park. We sat and watched the grounds crew take up the bases and begin preparing the field for the following day's game. And we kept talking about all of those home runs we had watched soaring over the fence. We were still talking about the homers, as well as the 30 runs we saw cross the plate, when we devoured plates of Southern barbeque for supper and even when the lights were out and our heads were on pillows late that night. It had been quite a day.

The fireworks continued Sunday. Robertson slugged two more home runs and knocked in six runs as Pittsburgh won another slug-fest, 10-7. Robertson hit four homers in three days, lifting his total to 15. Jeter homered and drove in the other four runs for the Pirates. Aaron clouted another home run and had four RBI. The ninth inning provided additional thrills.

In the top of the inning, Hoyt Wilhelm came in to pitch for the

Braves. He was forty-eight years old, only two years younger than my dad. Known for throwing one of the best knuckleballs of all time, Wilhelm threw pitches that dipped, dove, and fluttered, while batters flailed away helplessly. He set the Pirates down without a run. When he finished his career just shy of his fiftieth birthday, Wilhelm had pitched in 1,070 games and owned a brilliant 2.52 career earned run average. He was the first relief pitcher to be inducted into the Hall of Fame.

In the bottom of the ninth, the Braves again hit back-to-back homers as Jimmie Hall and Mike Lum connected. It was the third time in two days we had seen successive batters hit home runs.

We did not hang around after that game. We hit the road and headed back to Fayetteville, spending most of the trip rehashing the two games we had seen. Dad and I had always re-played baseball games, going back to the ones I took part in, from Little League on up. We sure had a lot to talk about in the car: 13 home runs, 47 runs, 65 hits. Other than my daddy dozing for thirty or so minutes, the drive of more than six hours was filled with our verbal replays.

Over the nearly two decades that followed, Dad accompanied me to numerous games in Atlanta. We invited various friends to go with us at different times, and my older daughter, Erika, joined Dad and me the last few years that he went. That was extra special for him, watching big league baseball with his granddaughter.

I know he enjoyed himself on those trips. We saw most of the other National League teams play the Braves. We were thrilled to see Willie Mays hit a home run and make a couple of his patented basket catches. We were practically mesmerized watching Bob Gibson mow down the Atlanta hitters. We were excited to see Lou Brock steal a base. We always loved it when Hank Aaron smashed home runs, and we saw him smash quite a few of them. We watched the Big Red Machine, with Johnny Bench, Joe Morgan, and Pete Rose. During a weekend series, Bench popped two home runs, Morgan hit one and swiped a base, and Rose did one of his patented belly-flop slides into second as he stretched a single into a double.

In 1976, the Braves brought up a twenty-year-old catcher named Dale Murphy. He was tall, six-foot-five, and gangly, and he looked too tall to be a catcher. My daddy liked him instantly. It wouldn't be long before everyone liked Murphy. He did not remain behind the plate for long, moving to first base for a while and eventually to the outfield. He won five consecutive Gold Gloves playing center field and a pair of MVP trophies. And he was a nice person, one of those guys any parent would want his son to be like.

Murphy's arrival was significant for Dad and me because it signaled a shift in our team loyalties. Both of us jumped from the Pirates to the Braves. It was not a case of latching onto a frontrunner; Atlanta lost at least 92 games from 1975-79, finishing more than 40 games out of first place one of those years. The Braves had above-.500 records three times in a four-year stretch before turning terrible once more, averaging 96 losses from 1985-90. For several seasons, Murphy was about all that Braves fans had to cheer about.

Then, something wonderful happened. Three young pitchers — Tom Glavine, Steve Avery, and John Smoltz — blossomed, and the Atlanta Braves became a good team. So good that they vaulted from worst to first. After finishing in last place in their division in 1990, they were on top in 1991. They went on to win the National League pennant and play in the World Series. That year started a run of fourteen division titles in a row for the Braves.

Dad and I witnessed the transformation as it unfolded. On July 29 of 1991, we arrived in Atlanta for the Braves' series with Pittsburgh. It was to have been a three-game set, but a rainout earlier in the season resulted in a doubleheader being scheduled for the first day of the Pirates' visit. That was a Monday, and over 32,000 fans were at Fulton County Stadium — a pretty good crowd for a Monday.

The Braves took the first game of the doubleheader and won the second on back-to-back home runs from Francisco Cabrera and Mark Lemke. It was the first homer of the season for each of them. Atlanta won again Tuesday and swept the four-game series with a Wednesday victory keyed by three-run home runs in the fifth inning by Deion Sanders and Jeff Blauser. Barry Bonds had a three-run shot for the Pirates.

I remember thinking that Bonds might have been the best all-around player in the major leagues. I continued to feel that way, although I soured on Bonds when it seemed apparent that he was using steroids to bolster his production. I never understood why someone so talented would risk his reputation, not to mention his health, in order to hit home runs. I guess it shows just how caught up everyone became with the long ball.

It was a couple of years later when I realized our baseball trips to Atlanta had become more work than fun for my daddy. We always stayed at a little motel on Pollard Street, not far at all from Fulton County Stadium. The walk from the ball park to the motel was maybe three or four blocks, but there was a small hill to climb along the way. I noticed Dad was struggling, and as I made sure he was okay, it dawned on me that he was seventy-three years old. The Georgia heat was suffocating, and that, combined with everything else, was taking a huge toll on him. Dad didn't complain, but on Sunday — the day of the final game of the series and our trip — I noticed that he seemed more relieved than excited when he reached his seat at the stadium. On the way home, it was easy to see he was worn out. I knew that would be his last baseball trip.

The following year, I offered Dad the chance to join me for some Braves games. I was almost afraid he would say yes. Afraid because I didn't know what might happen if he went. He looked at me when I mentioned two or three possible dates for the trip, and I saw sadness in his eyes where there once had been a spark upon the prospect of taking a baseball road trip. Dad said he thought he would sit it out that year and just watch the games on TV.

I felt a sense of relief and sadness, too. Then, perhaps to prevent himself from drowning in the disappointment of the present, Dad started talking about our very first trip to see the Braves play and about all of the home runs we watched being belted over the fences at Fulton County Stadium. It brought back happy memories, and we both shared those kinds of thoughts for an hour or so.

And those types of recollections are the ones Dad and I continued to share.

Chapter 20
Baseball is Back in Town

Our city gets a minor league team

Wes Westrum, a catcher who played his entire eight-year major league career with the New York Giants, said it well: "Baseball is like church. Many attend, but few understand."

From the time I was about twelve years old, I grew irritated with people who said baseball was too slow-moving, that it bored them. They were bored because they did not understand baseball. They just didn't get it. Didn't get that it is more than a sport and that it is not just a game. It is The Game. While baseball players may not possess the athleticism of, say, a Michael Jordan, they must be tremendous all-around athletes. I feel baseball players are the best rounded of all athletes because so much is required of them: throwing, fielding, running, making the correct plays, and hitting (remember, many feel hitting a round ball with a round bat and hitting it squarely is the most difficult thing to do in all of sport). Being tall or massively muscular does not help; being small is not a detriment. There are so many nuances, and someone who really loves baseball knows those intricacies, understands it is more than simply throwing and hitting a ball. Much more.

Sure, baseball takes time to play, and there are lulls when there is no action. But the fact that time is not of the essence is one of the game's most endearing qualities. You can't dribble out the clock or take a knee. You have to get that last out. Sooner or later, you have to throw the ball over the plate. As for the slow pace, I like it. Maybe that's because I'm from the South, where everything moves a little slower.

I enjoy imagining what is being discussed in those meetings at the mound or guessing what the managers' next moves will be: bunt, hit and run, pitch-out? I enjoy sitting there while a pitching coach goes to the mound or while a reliever walks in from the bullpen. It gives me time to try and think along with the managers, to consider possible strategies from both dugouts.

I do not leave baseball games early. Never. There is always the possibility I might miss something. Maybe one of the teams will pull off a triple play. Or someone will hit a grand slam. Perhaps one of those once-in-a-lifetime freaky plays will occur. But aside from that, until the last out has been recorded, there is still baseball to be played. And I love baseball.

I love it at all levels. So, I was overjoyed to learn in late 1986 there was a possibility that our city would be getting a minor league baseball team. It had been thirty years since professional baseball was played in Fayetteville. The prospect of having a pro team to follow, with games played nearby all through the summer, was a happy one.

The rumor became reality during the winter months, and even though the local team owners were pushed to the brink to meet the deadline, everything was in place when spring of 1987 rolled around. The Fayetteville Generals were a single-A affiliate of the Detroit Tigers, and their manager was to be former big league shortstop Johnny Lipon. Building a stadium proved the greatest obstacle, and it took a rush job by financiers and construction workers to have it ready in time.

I was eager to be involved with the Generals in some way, so I was happy to get the job as the official scorer for home games. I had left the newspaper two years earlier, wanting to spend more time with our daughter. I loved covering college basketball, but that sport caused me to be away from home several nights a week during the season. I believed I could make a good living as a free-lance writer, working at home and making my own schedule. It took a while to cultivate contacts with enough magazines and other publications for which to write, but it worked out well. I was able to earn a steady source of income with a full-time part-time job with a local radio station. I went in every weekday morning around 4:30 and prepared and delivered seven brief news and sports summaries each day. The station signed a contract with the Generals to broadcast all of their home games, and I served as the color commentator.

It didn't take long to find that keeping the scorebook and offering observations about the game were too much to do at the same time. I gave up the scorekeeping and continued the radio work, enjoying it immensely. I assisted in the play-by-play, and I produced and recorded a pre-game show for each game. The best part of that was getting to know Lipon, who was a frequent guest on what we called the Generals' Dugout Show. He willingly agreed to interviews whenever I asked him, and he corralled players to be on my show.

Even better, though, was the relationship we built. Lipon could tell that I was in love with baseball, just as he had been his whole life. I would hang around the stadium sometimes when I was not preparing for a game, and we would sit in the dugout. Lipon would get a faraway gaze in his eyes, like he was staring into his past, and he told story after story about his playing days and some of the great players he came to know. I never tired of hearing the stories, and he never tired of telling them.

Minor league baseball has a certain intrigue. It has to do with players who will one day play in the big leagues. Some are so obvious in their ability that anyone who has followed the game much at all can recognize that barring injury, they will make it. Others are works in progress and surprise fans when their names appear one day in major league box scores.

Travis Fryman was the best Generals player to reach the majors. A shortstop in Fayetteville, he went on to spend thirteen years in big leagues. He played for the Detroit Tigers and Cleveland Indians, converting to third base where he won a Gold Glove. Fryman was a five-time All-Star who hit 223 home runs and drove in 1,022 runs during his career. After hitting no home runs in 411 at-bats with Fayetteville, he smacked 20 or more homers seven times.

Watching Fryman and players like him on other teams in the South Atlantic League — the best-known of those early days was Asheville's Craig Biggio, and later, there was Chipper Jones — and then following their path to the majors was somehow gratifying, kind of like being a part of their rise to glory. But, as usual, just being around the grass, dirt, and chalk lines of a baseball field and witnessing the games was the biggest treat of all. Sitting behind the microphone was enjoyable because I was talking about baseball, and that was easy. I just described what I saw and explained why certain things happened. I did it in a plain-spoken way, talking as I would when discussing the game with a friend.

Going down on the field prior to games gave me a charge. It was exhilarating being that close to everything, hearing the catcher's mitt pop while a pitcher warmed up close by and appreciating how smoothly infielders gobbled up ground balls and threw effortlessly to first during their pre-game preparation. Sometimes I would venture into the dugout and pick up a bat to get the feel of it. If it was a long time before game time, I might step outside and take a few swings in the summer air. Boy, that sure felt good.

Once, the Generals brought in Bob Feller to help put some fannies in the seats. A member of the Hall of Fame and one of the best ambassadors the game of baseball has ever had, the former Cleveland Indians' pitcher had thrown what was known as serious smoke before radar guns had come along. Those who had seen him said his fastball would have been clocked at more than 100 miles per hour.

When he came to Fayetteville, Bullet Bob was seventy years old, and he had not pitched professionally for thirty-two years. He was still in great shape, and he had obviously kept his trusty right arm in shape, too.

Before the Generals' game that evening, Feller took the mound at Riddle Stadium. Media representatives were invited to go up to the plate and take a swing against him. He walked out there, wearing soft-soled shoes, tossed three or four balls from in front of the mound to loosen up, then toed the rubber and threw a couple much harder pitches.

I was eager to at least stand in the batter's box against the great Bob Feller. Some of the Generals' players offered a half-dozen of their discard bats for us to use. I remember that another radio guy, who wanted to bat first, was looking around for a helmet. When Feller realized what the delay was about, he shouted, "Don't anybody worry about getting hit. Every pitch I throw will be a strike, or close to it."

Feller was true to his word. His right arm shot one pitch after another across home plate. The first few batters, including two newspaper writers and a radio station executive, watched balls zip into the catcher's mitt. Feller walked halfway to the plate, and, being the gentleman he is, said in a low voice, "We don't have a long time, so be swinging the bats, men. I'll throw the ball in there, and you fellows take a rip."

Three straight batters swung and missed, and Feller gave them all a second chance, which they also whiffed. The guy before me hit a dribbler toward shortstop. I had made up my mind to try to get the bat out in front so the ball would not blaze past me. I was able to do that, timing a pitch which was waist-high, right down the middle. I hit the ball on a soft line into right field; it would have been a clean single. Feller suggested that I try another one, and I hit that pitch harder, into center field.

I tried not to show how tickled I was as I walked back to the dugout to the cheers of the Generals. I waited around about five minutes, until everyone had batted, so I could meet Bob Feller. When he walked off the field, I shook his hand and introduced myself. He smiled, patted me on the back, and said, "Those were nice swings you put on those balls. Good going."

It was not real competition, and I know that, even at the age of seventy, this legendary pitcher could have thrown the ball past me had he so desired. But hitting two of Bob Feller's pitches into the outfield ranks among my proudest sports accomplishments.

Chapter 21
Minor League Memories

An old yellow baseball and
Mr. Twenty-Seven

I have this old baseball. It has turned a yellowish color despite being stored in a plastic bag, but you can still make out the names even though they were signed more than fifty years ago.

The autographs of Danny Osinski and Wynn Hawkins stand out partly because both pitchers made it to the major leagues, but also because they "adopted" a small boy who idolized them. Jim Pokel was the most popular local autograph back then, and my daddy and other men who knew baseball talked a lot about an infielder named Donnie Montgomery.

Those names and others scrawled on my treasured ball were listed on the roster of the Fayetteville Highlanders. I was nine years old when the 1956 Carolina League season began. My daddy worked at a tire store, and one of the co-owners had purchased two season tickets to support the team. But he didn't care much for baseball, and knowing that Dad loved it, he gave the tickets to him.

Dad and I attended every regular-season game at Pittman Stadium. It was located where an automobile dealership now sits. I heard people say how the stadium was rickety and in need of major repairs, but I thought it was heaven. The summer of '56 was special. My daddy and I went to every single game during regular season, and we stayed until the last out was recorded in every one of those games.

The best player I saw was Curt Flood of High Point-Thomasville. The Hi-Toms' center fielder was so fast that it seemed he could catch everything from foul line to foul line. He slammed home runs, hit for average, and stole bases. The future St. Louis Cardinals' star was just plain amazing. Eventual Hall of Famer Willie McCovey played first base for Danville, and his teammate, outfielder Leon Wagner, belted 51 home runs that season. He also made it to majors.

Hawkins and Osinski paid me a lot of attention. My daddy and I sat behind the Fayetteville dugout, which was between home plate and first base. The Highlanders' bullpen was a little way down the right field line. I became a frequent visitor to the bullpen, standing by the fence and talking to the two pitchers when they were not on the mound.

They answered my endless questions about how to be a pitcher, what hitters on the team did when they were in slumps, which teammates had the best shot at making it to the big leagues, and anything else I could think to ask. Each would slip me a baseball every now and then, and I think both enjoyed the fact that I was in love with the game they played for a living. Osinski and Hawkins were like pals.

Pokel was the Highlanders' glamour boy. A muscular first baseman with dark hair and good looks, the left-handed slugger blasted long home runs and had a flair for the dramatic. He might strike out four times and then launch a game-winning homer in the ninth inning. Pokel was strong, and he swung hard. He looked the part of the home run hitter that he was.

Montgomery was one of those guys who just looked like a ball player. You watched him trot onto the field, and you knew he was good. He was thin and loose, his head bobbing when he ran. He was a smooth fielding shortstop, and he could hit, especially in the clutch, and he was the Highlanders' most consistent batter. Hawkins told me that Montgomery would have been in the big leagues if not for an injury that permanently weakened his throwing arm. When that arm bothered him, he would play first base or even second. Manager Dutch Meyer wanted to keep Montgomery's bat in the lineup.

I remember Ed Cook was a terrific center fielder who hit nearly thirty home runs. Dick Hofleit in right field and Glenn Phillips in left also had some power at the plate. Hofleit and Cook both possessed rifle arms that nailed runners at third base and home.

Osinski and Hawkins were outstanding pitchers, and so was Larry Dresen, who led the Highlanders in wins. All three were right-handers.

Fayetteville finished in fourth place during the regular season, then knocked off High Point and Danville in the playoffs to win the Carolina League championship.

I was thrilled for my heroes, except for the fact that I missed the last two home victories as the Highlanders won the title in the middle of September. I had my tonsils taken out and was in the hospital for two days.

When Hawkins and Osinski saw my daddy at the last game without me, they asked where I was. Dad told them, and the pitchers got a ball signed by everyone on the Fayetteville team. They brought it to me in the hospital, and I cried.

As it turned out, that was the final game ever played at Pittman Stadium and the final game for the Highlanders. It would be thirty-one years before minor league baseball returned to Fayetteville. The team folded after winning the championship.

Years later, when plans for the Fayetteville Generals were unfolding, folks recollected that huge crowds had attended games at Pittman Stadium in 1956. That wasn't so. The attendance figures were low until playoff time, and the crowds weren't enormous even then.

As a small boy, I didn't know anything about baseball being a business and could not believe there would not be a team in Fayetteville the year after my beloved Highlanders had won it all.

I have wonderful memories of the summer of '56. I will never forget Wynn Hawkins and Danny Osinski and how kind they were to me. The joy of those nights at the ball park still lingers. But so does the sadness of not getting to do it again in 1957.

My old yellowish baseball would not get any attention on eBay. But, then, I would never put it up for auction anyway. No one has enough money to buy it.

My wife, Dahlia, and I have two daughters. Erika, the older one, liked baseball. Laura always loved it. She was born in 1987, the year the Fayetteville Generals became our city's first pro baseball team in thirty-one years. By the time she was four, we were going to games together.

When she was six, Laura and I attended a home game at Riddle Stadium one night and were sitting in the bleachers down the right field line. She mentioned early in the game that she wanted to get a foul ball. When Laura said something like that, she meant that she wanted to do it herself; she wasn't asking me to get a ball for her.

Over the first few innings, five or six foul balls were hit in our direction, landing in a large dirt area behind the bleachers. Laura sprinted after each one, and each time, she came back empty-handed. The last time, looking a bit dejected, Laura said, "Those boys are bigger than me, and I can't beat them to the balls."

It was maybe an inning later when she got up from her seat, and saying nothing to me, walked down to fence which separated the Generals' bullpen from a walkway in front of the bleachers. Fayetteville's relief pitchers sat on a bench with their backs against the fence. Laura stuck her little fingers through the fence and tapped a pitcher who wore the number twenty-seven on his back.

I was sitting fairly close, and I heard what she said: "Mr. Twenty-Seven, I want to get a baseball. I have tried for some foul balls tonight, but there are a lot of boys going for them, too, and they are bigger and faster than me. So, I haven't got one. Mr. Twenty-Seven, would you get me a baseball?"

"Mr. Twenty-Seven" was a left-handed pitcher named Matt Bauer. He turned to listen to my daughter, and he smiled at this blue-eyed, curly-haired fan who had both nerve and imagination. Without hesitation, he said, "Sure, I'll get you a ball. I can't do it while the game is going on, but after it's over, if you will wait right here, I'll bring you a baseball."

Laura told him thank you and was beaming when she returned to sit beside me. "Mr. Twenty-Seven is going to get me a baseball," said Laura, not doubting for a second that it would happen.

Bauer warmed up and pitched the ninth inning, earning a save as he preserved a one-run Generals lead. Following the last out, he received congratulations from all of his teammates and then was interviewed by a sports writer from the local newspaper. I started to wonder if maybe, in all the excitement, if Mr. Twenty-Seven might forget his promise.

But he did not. He walked down to where Laura was standing patiently waiting by the fence, told her he had to go to the club house to get a ball, and then he would come back and give it to her. He did just that.

Matt Bauer won six games that season and saved five others. He would climb as high as Triple-A before his baseball career ended at the age of twenty-five.

I have no idea what his fondest baseball memory is. I do know that he provided a little girl one of her fondest memories. Laura will always remember Mr. Twenty-Seven.

Chapter 22
A Few Minutes with Dale

An interview with baseball's all-time Mr. Nice Guy

Dale Murphy was one of the most popular Atlanta Braves of all time, mostly because he was one of baseball's premier handful of players for a stretch and also because he was one of the nicest guys on earth.

He did not swear, fuss with umpires, charge the pitcher's mound, throw bats, beat up water coolers, or criticize teammates or opponents. The only person he got mad at was himself, and even then, he seldom showed it.

Murphy was always genuinely humble, an unassuming and shy guy who seemed surprised by all the attention showered upon him. He was the main attraction in Atlanta for several summers in the 1980s. And not just Atlanta. He won back-to-back National League Most Valuable Player awards in 1982 and '83.

Off the field, he lived the kind of life most of us wish we lived. He was always doing something for someone, visiting sick kids and helping someone in need. He felt it was a privilege to serve others. In 1987, he was honored by *Sports Illustrated* as one of Eight Athletes Who Care, each designated as Sportsman of the Year by the magazine.

Murphy put together a string of superb seasons for the Braves. His 1982 MVP numbers included a .281 batting average, 109 RBI, 113 runs scored, and 23 stolen bases. It was the first of three straight seasons in which he hit 36 home runs. The next year, he batted .302, driving in 131 runs, scoring 121, and stealing 30 bases in a repeat MVP performance. He smacked 44 homers in 1987 and finished his career with 398. He was a Gold Glove center fielder from 1982-86 and was in the National League All-Star team's starting outfield all five of those years.

On Friday, July 5, 1985, my dad and I left Fayetteville for our annual trip to Atlanta to see a weekend of Braves games. I had obtained a press pass, mainly with the idea of talking with Murphy. The Mets were in town, and the night before we arrived, the teams played a marathon. Rain delays and nineteen innings delayed the July Fourth fireworks display until after 3 a.m.

Walking through the clubhouses of both teams, I could tell all of the Mets and Braves were very tired. No one had gotten enough sleep, and everyone looked bleary-eyed. I didn't see Murphy anywhere. I asked one of the Braves' locker room attendants, and he said Murphy was doing some hitting underneath Fulton County Stadium. So I waited.

The locker room emptied, with players going out onto the field to throw and get loose. Finally, Murphy appeared. His right hand was wrapped, the result of getting jammed with a pitch the previous night. He had been hitting under the stands in order to test the hand. Some players would have sat out that night. Murphy told me he was going to play.

I asked if I could talk with him for a few minutes, and the seven-time All-Star said, "Well, I have to do several television and photo sessions before the game, and those people are out there now. But I can give you a couple minutes while I change shoes."

A couple was better than nothing, and I started asking my questions, most of which dealt with the huge expectations Murphy faced. Fans expected him to produce in every clutch situation, and they, along with many other people, expected him to meet requests for autographs, appearances, and hospital visits.

"I have trouble saying no," he told me. "It isn't a matter of trying to be a nice guy as much as wanting to do things for people. I know fans like to talk with players and get their autograph. I understand writers have stories to do, that people want to talk to me. In the past, I have taken too much time from my family trying to meet most of the requests. It detracted from my family life. Now, I'm trying to say no sometimes. But, I have to admit, when I do, I feel kind of guilty. I want to cooperate, but I cannot give people all my time. I'll do whatever I can."

When I spoke with Braves officials, I learned that Murphy's "whatever I can" usually translated into filling nearly every request and that he never refused one involving a sick child.

Because Murphy had enjoyed several outstanding seasons, fans and writers seemed to expect him to come through with the big hit every time. That he had started the 1987 season on fire — hitting .380 with nine home runs and a record-equaling 29 RBI in April — did not help any. When he cooled off, critics came out of the woodwork.

"That start was a little bit of a curse," he said. "People expected me to keep it up, and that's impossible. I'm realistic enough to know you are going to have your hot times and your cold times. It's a long season. Still, sometimes I put pressure on myself; we all do. I have times I try too hard, but it's not drastic. I probably expect more from myself than my manager or teammates do."

Even during bad days and slumps, Murphy did not lose his temper.

"Well, there was one time last season when I kicked a water cooler," he said sheepishly. "And I regretted it. I have shown anger before, but it doesn't work for me. Some guys break loose and get their feelings out, and it helps. Not me. I get frustrated and upset, but when I get mad, it just means I'm losing control and my ability to keep cool.

"That's what you've got to do. It's important to keep myself under control so I can concentrate. When I let it get to me, it hurts my concentration. It's better for me not to be so up and down emotionally, but rather to remain at an even keel. And not just to set a good example."

Much was written about Murphy doing just that, about his being the closest thing to a perfect role model.

"Those are nice compliments," he said, "but they have been done to the extent that people lose touch with reality. I just try to be myself. I want to be kind to people, and I live and act the way I do because that's what I think is right. But it's not like I don't have things that are faults in my life. I appreciate what people say and write, but it gets to be embarrassing. No one is like some people think I am. I'm not perfect."

I thanked Murphy for his time, and he looked up from the stool he was sitting on and asked, "Are you sure you got enough? Are there any other questions?"

After promising me a couple of minutes, he had given me fifteen, even though he was pressed for time. He had gone out of his way for someone he didn't even know.

But, then, the fact that he cared about people and was always so kind was one of the reasons Dale Murphy was so special.

Chapter 23
Baseball Road Trips with My Daughter

Laura and I visit Cooperstown and
make a five-city big league junket

Our daughters, Erika and Laura, took an early interest in baseball. I'm sure my love for the game had more than a little to do with that. Erika played quite a bit of softball and was an exceptional hitter. Laura played baseball as long as she could and then became an exceptional pitcher in fast-pitch softball. But she always wished she could have continued playing baseball.

Erika, who is five and a half years older than Laura, went with my dad and me to some Braves games in Atlanta. Before long, both girls were going with me for a weekend series every year. As she became a teenager, Erika lost interest in baseball; at least, she no longer wanted to travel to Atlanta to see games. So Laura and I went. Year after year after year. For thirteen consecutive seasons, we drove down on a Friday, attended a night game, watched an afternoon or night game Saturday, and returned home following a Sunday afternoon contest.

Laura was an enthusiastic fan, not just of the Braves, but of baseball. She soaked up statistics and knowledge of the game and its players. She became a student of the game and quite the little historian. Probably because I particularly loved the major leagues in the late 1950s and throughout the 1960s, so did Laura. She knew about Warren Spahn and all of his 20-win seasons and multitudes of complete games. She talked about Bill Mazeroski turning the double play and Roberto Clemente making unbelievable throws to nail runners.

Our baseball road trips were filled with conversations about what was going on currently with our Braves as well as "old days" baseball stuff. Unless we got held up by construction work on I-95 or I-20 (and that happened more than a few times), we pulled into our motel in mid-afternoon on Friday. It was a short walk to Fulton County Stadium, and when Turner Field opened in 1997, we stayed right across the street from the ball park. Laura and I were almost always standing at the gates when they opened. We wanted to soak in every bit of baseball that we could.

Batting practice was usually taking place when we arrived. The Braves would hit first, followed by the visiting team. Our normal perch for BP was in right field, on the very first row. We stood near the Atlanta bullpen so we could watch Greg Maddux, John Smoltz, or whichever pitcher in the rotation who was throwing between starts. Laura, who has never been shy, was bold enough to ask players and coaches for baseballs. And they frequently complied. In fact, she brought home at least one National League baseball eight years in a row. Twice, she got two. Braves pitching coach Leo Mazzone gave her a ball two different times.

One year, we found out that Braves players would sometimes sign autographs before and after games behind Turner Field. There was a fenced-in area where the players, coaches, and manager Bobby Cox parked their cars and trucks. On the other side of the fence was a sidewalk, and fans would line up all along the fence, waiting for a member of the Atlanta team to drive up. When one of them got out of his car, everyone would yell out, begging whoever it was to please sign their baseball, scrap of paper, bat, shirt, or hat. Most of players ignored the pleas; after all, they heard that stuff all the time and they grew tired of it.

Occasionally, though, a player would wander over and sign for a while. Laura always carried one of the baseballs she had been given during batting practice sessions, and when she was able to get an autograph on a ball, she was ecstatic. She never jumped up and down or anything, but I could see the excitement in her eyes. Over the years, she got balls signed by Chipper Jones, Tom Glavine, and Braves broadcaster Don Sutton, a Hall of Fame pitcher. Cox signed on two balls. Laura even got Andruw Jones twice. That was no small accomplishment since he very seldom signed for anybody. One of those times, she was the only person standing outside the fence when Jones stepped out of his silver sports car. She had checked with the parking lot attendant to make sure Jones had not arrived. When told that he had not, she waited and waited, while I stood in the background. He walked straight from his car over to where Laura stood, signed her baseball, and thanked her for being so patient to stand for so long.

Smoltz has always been Laura's favorite player. There were many, many times that we stood for an hour or two, hoping she could obtain an autograph. We never saw Smoltz or Maddux sign once. Laura did get Smoltz's autograph, and he posed while I took a picture of him beside her. She was one of hundreds in line, donating canned goods to the Atlanta food bank in an effort to help feed the hungry. Smoltz did that every year.

Laura and I stood in line together, and neither of us minded one bit. She counts that signature and picture as treasures. Another prized autograph came from Ozzie Smith, the acrobatic shortstop who is a member of the Hall of Fame. It proved to be quite a surprise.

A week or so before the 1999 World Series between the Atlanta Braves and New York Yankees, Braves broadcaster Skip Caray announced while doing a game on the radio that Series tickets could be bought by calling a certain phone number. He gave the day and time when the tickets would go on sale. Laura suggested I give it a try. I was reluctant, saying it would be a waste of time and that I would never get through to get tickets, but she insisted that it was worth a try.

So, on the appointed date, I began dialing. Busy signal … over and over again. Just what I expected. That's all I thought I would hear. But, after about twenty minutes, there was a ring, and a recorded voice told me to wait for the chance to place an order for World Series tickets. I bought four, and Laura, Erika, Dahlia, and I were part of the Turner Field crowd of over 51,000 for Game One. It was October 23, a Saturday night, and it was freezing cold. The temperature at game time was forty-nine degrees, and there was a breeze. We all wore sweaters, winter coats, and gloves, and we froze. I don't know how cold it was by the time the game ended almost three hours later.

Chipper Jones hit a solo home run off Orlando Hernandez in the fourth inning, and Maddux made the run stand up by pitching shutout baseball until the eighth. That's when the roof caved in, as the first four Yankees to bat in the inning reached base and came around to score. Atlanta made some noise in the bottom of the ninth with a walk and single, bringing the tying run to the plate. But Hall-of-Famer-to be Mariano Rivera slammed the door.

After the game, Erika and Dahlia headed back to the motel across the street, anxious to get some feeling back into their fingers and toes. Laura and I walked around to the parking area in hopes that she could secure some autographs. Understandably, none of the Braves' players were in the mood to sign. We started to walk away when I spotted Ozzie Smith, who had been working the game for a television outlet. I pointed him out to Laura, and she ran over to him with her ball and pen. He not only signed graciously, but thanked her for asking him and took a few minutes to chat with her.

Earlier in 1999, in August, Laura and I drove up to Cooperstown, New York, to visit the Baseball Hall of Fame. What a trip!

We stopped in Baltimore to see a game at Camden Yards. Detroit was in town, and the Tigers had four players who had spent time with our hometown club, the Fayetteville Generals. Our seats were barely in the ball park, on the back row of the left-field bleachers. That was fine with us. The setting, layout, and field at Camden Yards were all beautiful, with little juts and dips in the outfield wall mindful of old-time ball fields.

The Orioles won the game, 5-4, but two memorable moments for us had nothing to do with what happened on the playing field. During the game, the big scoreboard in center field at Camden Yards flashed the message that Wade Boggs had gotten his 3,000th hit. The previous day, Tony Gwynn had recorded number 3,000.

The night was hot, and Laura and I shared a tall lemonade, which was mighty refreshing. When we had drank all of the liquid, she put the chunk of lemon in her mouth. While sucking on it, she choked a little, and the lemon went shooting from her mouth like a rocket. It landed right on top of a man sitting in front of us. I froze in disbelief ... and a bit of fear, because the man appeared to frequent the weight room. Laura tried to stifle laughter, and we both sat, awaiting the reaction. Strangely enough, the man did not flinch. What was stranger, though, was that the man beside him — the two were looking at each other while engaged in conversation — did not do or say anything, either. It was as if that lemon slice was invisible.

That happened about the middle of the game, I think it was the sixth inning. That lemon stayed right there on the man's head the rest of the game, and neither he nor his friend ever gave any indication that they knew it was there. We certainly were not about to tell them. When the game ended, we did not tarry like we do sometimes; we bolted quickly down those steps.

The Hall of Fame was fantastic. As far as Laura and I were concerned, it was one of the Seven Wonders of the World. I had been there once before, thirty-eight years earlier when I was fifteen. I did not remember a lot. We spent two days, slowly taking in every exhibit. Laura read every single placard describing gloves, uniforms, bats, and other artifacts. The players' plaques were almost sacred to us. Just weeks before, Nolan Ryan, George Brett, Robin Yount, and Orlando Cepeda had been inducted, and we read about that. The first day, we bought some lunch and ate it while sitting in the stands at the ball park where the Hall of Fame game is played every year.

Upon entering the baseball shrine, the first thing one sees are statues of Babe Ruth and Ted Williams. They are the only statues in the place. I took a picture of Laura standing beside each one. We bought some post cards with players' plaques on the front. And we took a little time to browse the shops on the main street of town. A Roberto Clemente jersey caught Laura's eye, and I purchased that for her as she had great admiration for him — the way he played ball and lived his life.

Cooperstown is a quaint place. There are no chain restaurants or motels. The place we stayed was very old and not at all modern. But we didn't care, and I'm certain most visitors feel the same way. Everyone goes to soak in the baseball and share the chill bumps. We did our share of both.

Laura and I had talked about putting together an extended baseball road trip, one that would allow us to see games in several cities within a short period of time. Geography and scheduling were the keys, of course, to making it work. In 2008, we got serious. Six major league teams in the Midwest would be playing home games during a stretch in early August. Laura took care of reservations for accommodations, and we decided to buy tickets at the gate of each ball park.

We embarked on a trip which would take us to five cities and six stadiums in an eight-day period. Leaving on Friday, August 15, we drove all day and barely made it to Cincinnati's Great American Ballpark for the Reds' game with St. Louis. In the first inning, Ryan Ludwick doubled and scored on Rick Ankiel's 23rd home run, giving the Cardinals a 2-0 lead. Chris Dickerson led off the game for Cincinnati with the first big league home run of his career. The Cardinals won, 5-3, as Albert Pujols had three hits. The crowd of just over 26,000 would be the smallest in the six games we attended.

Our motel was within walking distance of the stadium, just was it was in Cleveland and Detroit. The next morning, we left for Cleveland and arrived well before game time. All we had to do was cross the street to enter Progressive Field, where we watched The Anaheim Angels nip the Indians, 4-3. John Lackey pitched six solid innings for the Angels, who took advantage of four Cleveland errors. Francisco Rodriguez earned his 47th save on the way to a major league-record 62.

Sunday's game in Detroit began a little after one o'clock, and the day was extremely hot. Our seats were good ones, on the lower level between the first-base dugout and the right-field foul pole. They were also directly in the sun. We baked until late in the game, when the sun sneaked behind the upper deck in back of us.

The Comerica Park field seemed so small, and the outfield fences appeared quite inviting. Baltimore's hitters agreed as they teed off for twenty-two hits and a 16-8 win. Melvin Mora and Luke Scott slugged two home runs apiece, and Aubrey Huff also connected for the Orioles. Mora added a pair of doubles, a single, and six RBI.

That night, we ate dinner at a place Laura had found out about on-line. Mario's was a short distance from our motel, so we drove over. The restaurant was really nice, and the food was delicious. Mario's was offering some "throwback" specials, enabling us to enjoy exquisite Italian dishes at very reasonable prices.

Chicago was our next stop, and we stayed there four nights. We rode the L train (the Chicago subway) from downtown to Comiskey Park II for the White Sox's Monday night game with Seattle. Carlos Quinten blasted his 35th home run, one of four hit by Chicago, and the White Sox won, 13-5. Ichiro Suzuki had three hits for the Mariners.

Thinking that getting tickets to Cubs games might be difficult, Laura and I rode the L to Wrigley Field the following morning. As it turned out, we had no problem at all. Because Wrigley tickets are in such high demand, I figured they would be pretty expensive, but that wasn't the case, either. We bought tickets for two Cubs games against the Reds, and both night's seats were excellent. Both of us get a big kick out of going into baseball memorabilia shops, and Wrigley was surrounded by lots of them. Each of us purchased a fitted Cubs cap.

That evening, Rich Harden pitched two-hit baseball for seven innings as the Cubs shut out Cincinnati, 5-0. When the sun went down, it was chilly. That was a good excuse to buy some nice baseball undershirts — grey with Cub blue sleeves — which we put on to make the evening more comfortable. Wednesday night, the Reds won, 2-1. Bronson Arroyo, who was the losing pitcher in the game we saw in Cincinnati, allowed only three hits over seven innings to pick up the victory.

Wrigley Field was Smithsonian. The ivy on the outfield walls was so green, the fans were so loud, and the air seemed so alive. Just the opposite of what we experienced in Cincinnati. The fact that the Cubs were running away with the Central Division, while the Reds were floundering, obviously had something to do with it. But I just felt a certain atmosphere in Wrigley that I think is always there.

Thursday was an off day. No ball game. No long drive to make. We took a tour of the Sears Building and visited the campus of the University of Chicago. Dinner was at Gibson's Steakhouse, and the food was out of this world. Laura and I shared a thick, juicy steak large enough to feed an army, and boy, was it tender. The garlic mashed potatoes were so creamy, they dissolved in our mouth; no chewing was required. The bread was so good, we could have made a meal out of that. The dessert choice was really tough. We went with carrot cake, and the serving was not a slice, it was a SLAB. The cake was delicious. We did not come close to polishing it off, so we carried what was left back to our hotel for the next morning's breakfast.

Our last stop was Milwaukee. Since there was no lodging close to Miller Park, we decided to get back on the road after the game and drive until we grew sleepy. Our seats were down the right-field line in the upper deck, on the front row. Laura and I both love hot dogs at the ball park, and we enjoyed one at every stadium. In Milwaukee, though, we had to try a bratwurst, so we bought one of those and a hot dog, sharing both.

The Miller Park crowd of 41,637 was the largest of the games on our trip. Both Wrigley games were announced as sellouts, with official numbers right at 41,000.

Mike Cameron and J.J. Hardy hit home runs for the Brewers in a 10-4 win over the Pittsburgh Pirates. After each homer, Milwaukee mascot Bernie Brewer propelled himself down a slide, landing in what is called a splash zone. Before the team moved into its new stadium in 2001, when it resided at old County Stadium, Bernie slid into a huge mug of beer. The political incorrectness of that prompted the change to a splash zone. Another highlight of Brewers home games is the sausage race. Five people dress as a bratwurst, Polish sausage, Italian sausage, hot dog, and chorizo, and they stage a comical race around the warning track of the ball park.

It was actually fun to be tangled in the parking lot traffic with thousands of other cars. That was a baseball experience we had not endured since we had always either stayed within walking distance of stadiums or taken some sort of rail system from our motel to the ball park and back.

Driving into the night, Laura and I replayed the game we had just seen. When we finally stopped in the wee hours of Saturday morning, both of us were on the brink of sleep as we pulled down the covers of our beds. The next day, winding from Wisconsin into Illinois and then Michigan, from state to state, we had plenty to talk about.

Watching a ball game in Wrigley Field had certainly been enjoyable. And it meant that Laura and I had attended games in all three of baseball grand cathedrals, Yankee Stadium and Fenway Park being the other two. Laura graduated from Boston College, and while there, she went to a very large number of Red Sox games. I have seen two games at Fenway, and I came away with much the same impression as the one left with me by Wrigley.

I am looking for another way of saying it, but there is no better word than atmosphere. I loved hearing Sweet Caroline in the eighth inning and Dirty Water following a Red Sox win. Looking out to left field and viewing the Green Monster as it looms over pitchers ... that is one of those things baseball lovers can appreciate much the same way an art lover might appreciate a simple brush stroke of Van Gogh or Rembrandt. The lone red seat in the right-field bleachers at Fenway commemorates a bomb launched by none other than Ted Williams. It traveled 502 feet, still the longest home run ever hit in the fabled ball yard.

As the hours and miles passed on the journey back to North Carolina, Laura and I re-lived our week of baseball. The recollections included obvious highlights such as home runs and defensive gems, and also the rather "everyday" stuff of baseball: the grace of various second basemen as they pivoted to turn double plays; pitchers' deliveries, some of them flowing like good poetry, some herky-jerky like the stop-start of a driver's ed rookie; running catches made by outfielders who moved with the swiftness and grace of antelope; infielders gobbling up ground balls like expensive vacuums; grounds crews smoothing infield dirt; and that sweet sound of the crack of the bat.

We talked about how we thoroughly enjoyed all of the games we attended, from the bright white lines being drawn down each baseline prior to the first pitch to the way eager hurlers stared in to their catchers for the signal of which pitch to throw.

I couldn't help thinking how the endless conversations my daughter and I were having were so much like the ones my daddy and I had shared years before. Names of players were different, and the number of stadiums in which Laura and I had seen games was much larger. But it was the same kind of banter. It was baseball talk between two people who truly loved The Game.

Counting minor and major league games, I cannot say how many baseball games Laura and I have attended together. We have never left a game early. No matter the score. No matter the weather. No matter the time. We have sat through rain delays of more than three hours. There have been games in which a team led by fourteen runs after eight innings. We always watched the ninth, right down to the twenty-seventh out. We didn't want to miss a thing.

Chapter 24
Extra Innings

It sure has been fun

These days, most of my baseball is experienced sitting beside a radio, just the way it was when I sat by my daddy in our living room more than fifty years ago. Another example of coming full circle, I suppose. A local station carries all of the Atlanta Braves' games, and I often listen to them while reading a book.

That is one of the nice things about listening to baseball rather than watching it on TV. It is easy to do something else and keep up with the game. I enjoy novels and, of course, I read a lot of baseball books, fact and fiction. David Halberstam's Summer of '49 and October 1964 are two of my favorites.

I still peruse box scores during the season, although admittedly not as thoroughly as I once did. I periodically read game reports, player features, and daily updates of several teams, and I almost always read extended coverage of the Braves. All of that is done online. Thanks to the Internet, I know what is going on in the major leagues day to day, and I enjoy the hot stove reports in the winter months ... the trade rumors and such.

Stored away in my mind are many beautiful memories associated with baseball. I considered it a privilege to watch:

* Bill Mazeroski turn a double play. "No Touch" could catch, pivot, and release in one motion,

   * Tom Seaver drop and drive. His mechanics were a pitching clinic.

   * Willie Stargell menacingly windmill his bat as he stared out at the mound awaiting a pitch.

   * Ichiro foul off pitch after pitch before guiding a single through the infield.

   * Ken Griffey Junior swing the bat.

   * Johnny Bench sit behind the plate and pluck pitches one-handed as if he were picking apples.

   * John Smoltz pitch. What a competitor.

   * Willie Mays. Enough said.

   * Hank Aaron. Ditto.

   * Roberto Clemente. The Great One.

There were several times that I had on-the-field press credentials in Atlanta, and I would stand at the batting cage and listen to players as they talked hitting and kidded one another. The sound of wood hitting cowhide (horsehide until 1974) was so distinct and clear. Nearby, a coach beat ground balls at infielders working to sharpen their trade. Being down there, with major league hitters parading into the batter's box to take their cuts, was enchanting. Walking across the plush grass and stopping in the on-deck circle, I did a bit of pretending, if only for a few moments.

Feelings are difficult to express. Mere phrases cannot do justice to what I feel for my wife and two daughters. The influence of music is overwhelming. Beatles music continues to amaze me. Words, in books and lyrics, are gifts. I am left grasping, however, when I try to describe what family and music and words mean to me.

Thad Mumau

Baseball has become a feeling for me. It is deep inside, a combination of players, ball yards, and feats I have seen, along with personal experiences. From cow pastures to audiences with Hall of Famers to road trips with my dad and daughters, they have all been wonderful. The feeling never goes away, and sometimes recollections of a game or a conversation from decades ago will come to mind.

Then, when the grass begins to turn green and the sky becomes somehow bluer, that feeling comes bubbling up and grows more alive.

It happens every year.

Bibliography

Books

Aaron, Hank, and Lonnie Wheeler. I Had a Hammer: The Hank Aaron Story. New York: HarperTorch, 1992.

Cramer, Richard Ben. What Do You Think of Ted Williams Now? New York: Simon and Schuster, 2002.

Dixon, Phil, and Hannigan, Patrick J. The Negro Baseball Leagues, a Photographic History. Mattituck, NY: Amereon House, 1992.

Finoli, David, and Ranier, Bill. The Pittsburgh Pirates Encyclopedia. Champaign, IL: Sports Publishing LLC, 2003.

Groat, Dick, and Surface, Bill. The World Champion Pittsburgh Pirates. New York: Coward-McCann, Inc., 1961.

Heaphy, Leslie A. The Negro Leagues, 1869-1960. Jefferson, NC: McFarland & Company, Inc., 2003.

Helyar, John. Lords of the Realm: The Real History of Baseball. New York: Villard Books, 1994.

Hogan, Lawrence D. Shades of Glory, The Negro Leagues and the Story of African-Americana Baseball. Washington, DC: National Geographic Society, 2006.

James, Bill. The New Bill James Historical Baseball Abstract. New York: Free Press, 2001.

Kahn, Roger. The Head Game, Baseball Seen from the Pitcher's Mound. New York: Harcourt, 2000.

Pietrusza, David, Silverman, Matthew, and Gershman, Michael. Baseball, The Biographical Encyclopedia. Kingston, NY: Total Sports Publishing, 2000.

Purdy, Dennis. The Team by Team Encyclopedia of Major League Baseball. New York: Workman Publishing Company, 2006.

Solomon, Burt. The Baseball Timeline. New York: DK Publishing, 2001.

Vecsey, George. Baseball: the History of America's Favorite Game. New York: Modern Library, 2006.

Online Websites

Baseball-reference.com